IRRAWADDY FLOTILLA

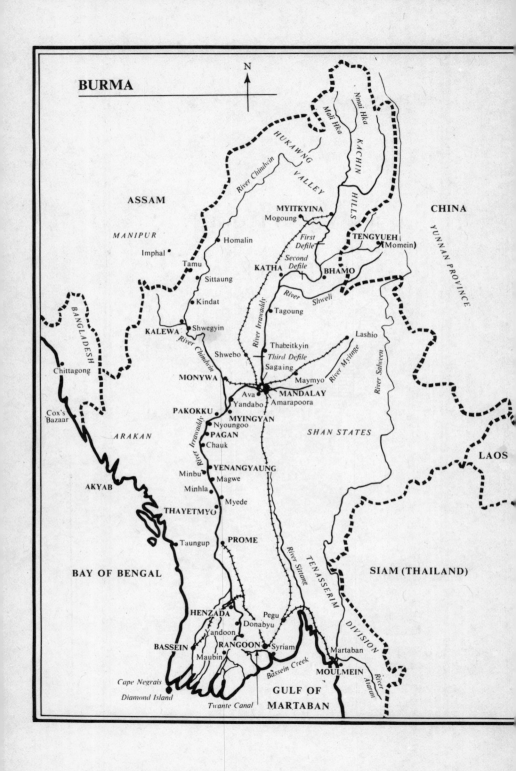

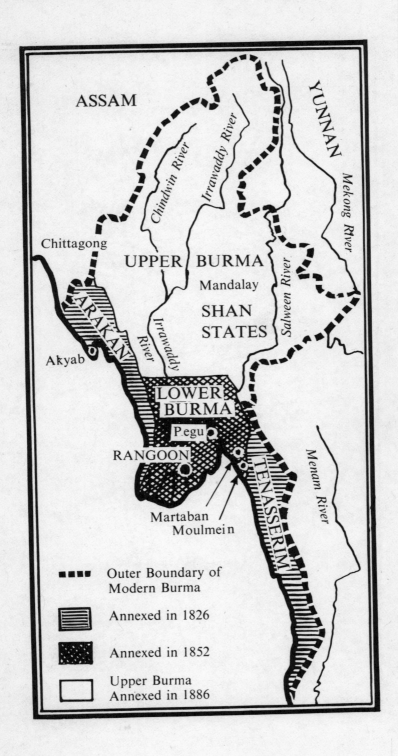

ASSAM

YUNNAN

Chindwin River

Irrawaddy River

Mekong River

Chittagong

UPPER BURMA

Mandalay

SHAN
STATES

Salween River

ARAKAN

Irrawaddy River

Akyab

LOWER
BURMA

Pegu

RANGOON

TENASSERIM

Menam River

Martaban
Moulmein

▪▪▪▪ Outer Boundary of
Modern Burma

Annexed in 1826

Annexed in 1852

Upper Burma
Annexed in 1886

IRRAWADDY FLOTILLA

BY ALISTER McCRAE AND ALAN PRENTICE

With a Foreword by
BERNARD FERGUSSON
(Lord Ballantrae)

"Come you back to Mandalay,
Where the old Flotilla lay:
Can't you 'ear their paddles chunkin'
From Rangoon to Mandalay?"

"I love the Burman with the blind
favouritism of first impression.
When I die I will be a Burman, with
twenty yards of real King's silk,
that has been made in Mandalay,
about my body."

from the works of Rudyard Kipling.

JAMES PATON LIMITED
18 Gordon Street
Paisley PA1 1XB

First Published 1978

Printed in Great Britain by James Paton Limited at Gazette Office, 18 Gordon Street, Paisley PA1 1XB

*To all those of whatever
race or creed who served
the "old Flotilla"*

Acknowledgements

The reader will find the Foreword by Bernard Fergusson of special interest. He and his wife Laura know Burma and the Irrawaddy and gave us the encouragement required to publish this book. We are very much indebted to them.

We have to thank the India Office Library & Records, the National Maritime Museum, the Royal Geographical Society and Glasgow's Mitchell Library for help so willingly given. Documents and books were produced for us which revealed how much there was to learn of our subject beyond our own personal experiences and knowledge acquired during our years in Burma.

Our thanks are due also to Mrs. John Carr (Dorothy Laird) whose advice on the research of a work of this kind was invaluable. She had a particular interest as the author of *Paddy Henderson,* which included a short account of the Irrawaddy Flotilla Company.

We have only ourselves to thank, or blame, for spellings adopted for the English versions of Burmese names and words; we have applied pure rule of thumb method. *Burma* itself was spelt *Burmah* up to some time in the late nineteenth century when the *h* seems to have gradually disappeared. But we have retained the *h* where we are quoting or in certain names, e.g. Burmah Oil Company.

Contents

Illustrations

Line Drawings — by J. C. Burnie

FOREWORD

By Bernard Fergusson

The Irrawaddy River comes into existence at a place called "The Confluence", some twenty miles north of Myitkyina. I have stood at The Confluence, and it is one of the most dramatic places in all the world. In a deep natural basin, a turbulent mountain torrent crashes into a placid lowland stream; and the waters thus mingled start on their long journey.

At the Confluence, or at that big sweep by the Government Rest-House (which used to be Steel Brothers') at Myitkyina, the mind's eye follows those waters as they flow, through mountains, hills and plains. They are reinforced from time to time, whether by minor streams humbly surrendering their identity, or by major rivers like the Shweli or the majestic Chindwin deigning to join forces. It sees too the River's progress through the three Defiles, of which the Second, between Bhamo and Katha, is the most dramatic: when the steamer appears to be approaching a solid and inexorable wall of rock as the River closes in. Suddenly a small cleft opens before you, and you are swept through a narrow channel, with cliffs towering above you on either side, and a small white pagoda half-way up on the starboard hand to wish you well. Soon you are through, with the long placid reaches ahead of you, and the sandbanks marked with little bits of tin flickering in the sunshine on bamboo poles. Then comes the long drift down to the Delta, with all the warmth, light, colour and movement; the activities on the bank at the steamer stations, with the vendors of rice and tea and the chickens running about; the tops of pagodas rising above the trees; the canoes, the fishing-boats, the long rafts with houses on them: all the things that come back to the mind's eye of those who love Burma. You pass great cities like Mandalay, and dead cities like Pagan. It is like moving along an artery.

I first saw the Irrawaddy in circumstances which were far from propitious, as a Column Commander on the First Wingate Expedition into Burma in March 1943. We reached it at a place called Tigyaing, thirty miles downstream from Katha, and I looked at it with awe: I had heard so much about it. We managed to cross it without too much trouble; but a month later, having suffered many casualties meanwhile, we were faced with the task of crossing back again, from the east bank to the west. My own small party eventually succeeded, near Moda, where Captain Redman was made prisoner in 1885 (see Chapter 10). Throughout those four weeks, the Irrawaddy had seemed hostile and malignant, for it was a truly formidable obstacle, with Japanese patrolling its banks, and confiscating all the canoes we had hoped to borrow.

But the Irrawaddy is by nature not hostile but benevolent; not an obstacle, but one of the great highways of the world. Since the dawn of time, the many different races who have inhabited Burma have paddled their way up and down it; and during the century or so that the British ruled that country (it was my great-grandfather, Lord Dalhousie, who annexed the Province of Pegu in 1852) it was first the Irrawaddy Flotilla in naval terms, and then the civilian Irrawaddy Flotilla Company, which provided a unique and historic service on the River, and on its principal tributary the Chindwin.

It was a magnificent Company. From its earliest days, it attracted men of the finest flower to serve both afloat and ashore. Most of those locally engaged came from Chittagong or Burma itself; most of those from overseas from Scotland: which, with Cornwall, was the source of most of the recruitment of the great British firms that built up Burma during that remarkable century. It was the young men of these firms with their early experience of taking responsible decisions who officered The Burma Rifles during the war, and I never in all my life encountered a finer lot of men. Another thing they had in common was a deep affection for that beautiful country and its wide variety of peoples, and they regarded the Irrawaddy with something like the veneration with which the ancient Egyptians regarded the Nile. Steel Brothers or Bombay Burmah, Burmah Oil or Macgregors or one of the smaller companies: these young men all had their loyalties and their pride and their friendly rivalries; but I suspect that those in the service of the Irrawaddy Flotilla Company had a certain secret satisfaction and swagger of their own. There is a glow in its very name.

Alister McCrae and Alan Prentice are typical of the breed that served the Company, and they were young enough to know it in its heyday. They were both educated at the High School of Glasgow, and both went out to Burma from that city: McCrae from the famous shipping office of Paddy Henderson in 1933, Prentice from Scottish Oils and Shell-Mex two years later. Each in turn served his apprenticeship as Cashier in the Head Office in Rangoon and on tour in the Irrawaddy delta before being appointed to the charge of an agency up-River. When war broke out in 1939 McCrae was Agent at Mandalay and Prentice at Bhamo. After the war, during which they both served in the Army, they took part in the Company's effort to restore the service, with McCrae as Deputy General Manager to Stuart Macdonald in Rangoon, and Prentice in McCrae's old job in Mandalay. The end of the story will be found in the Epilogue.

This book has been crying out loud to be written for many years past, and I am honoured to be launching it. Instead of bringing us down the River from the Confluence, the authors very rightly take us up it: so that we share something of the wonder with which the earliest European travellers beheld its revelations as they unfolded: as they were paddled north past Prome, and Myede, and Yenangyaung, and Magwe, and Pakokku, to Ava and Mandalay. I congratulate the reader on his good fortune, and wish him *bon voyage* as he embarks on that enchanting journey.

PART ONE

CHAPTER ONE

AN EMBASSY ON THE IRRAWADDY

The tides of the Irrawaddy delta ebb and flow fast and strong, and particularly this is so of the ebb in the high water season of the river. But when this high water ebb has reached its finality and is being held by the growing impact of the incoming flood tide, there is a period of slack water which will last for half an hour or more. In the wide Rangoon River the water lies apparently quite still during this period, awaiting the flood to make and carry away the flotsam brought down by the last ebb.

On the thirtieth of May 1795, while ships in Rangoon harbour were beginning to swing at their anchors to the early morning flood tide, a small fleet of country boats cast off one by one from the Ahlone shore at the north-east end of the city and were swept by their oarsmen into the still gentle current. The south-west monsoon had broken, but there was no rain; it was a humid and airless morning with the sun already reflecting a strong glare from the muddy water, a glare which pierces with blinding force into the eyes.

The boats were setting off on a 600 mile journey up the Irrawaddy River to Amarapoora, where the King of Burma, Bodawpaya, ruled over his dominions. The leading boat carried Captain Michael Symes of His Britannic Majesty's 7th Regiment, who had much to occupy his thoughts on the events of the past three months since he had sailed from Calcutta on this Mission to the Court of Ava.

The Governor-General of British India, Sir John Shore, had selected him to reopen diplomatic relations with the Burmese after an interval of thirty-three years. He was to be recognised as a highly accredited Envoy "deputed to lead an Embassy to the Kingdom of Ava". The reasons for the Embassy mainly arose from frontier incidents on the Arakan-Chittagong border in 1794 with constant risk of clashes between British and Burmese forces. Symes, then in his late thirties, was chosen "for his qualities in tact, courtesy and learning" and despatched post-haste to Burma.

Thus on 21st February 1795, *Seahorse,* an armed cruizer *(sic)* of the Bengal Marine (a squadron of the East India Company's navy) sailed from Calcutta with Captain Symes and the small staff and escort assigned to him. This comprised a British assistant-cum-secretary, a British doctor and sixteen Indian troops commanded by a Havildar (sergeant). After a call at the Andaman Islands they arrived at Rangoon on 21st March.

In his own account of the Embassy, Symes describes Rangoon as the most flourishing seaport in the Eastern world and "the Burman Empire second to China alone in power, of the Eastern Empires". He comments on the suitability of the Rangoon River for the construction of ships "the most favourable river in the world for naval architecture", several ships of 900 to 1000 tons burthen being seen on the stocks. Availability of teak from the Burma forests and spring tides with a rise of twenty feet provided Symes with good reasons for using such extravagant terms, and there was a further reason in the observation that the Burmese shipwrights were "athletic men, vigorous and industrious".

But arrival in Rangoon was not to be taken by this British Envoy as a signal for the Burmese to facilitate his progress to Amarapoora without delay. The Royal permission had first to be obtained and this took two months to secure, during which time Symes and his party cooled their heels on board *Seahorse.*

At last the Myowun (Governor) of the Province of Pegu, whose acquaintance Captain Symes had already made, announced that he had the King's orders to arrange for the British party to proceed up river and to accompany them himself. Symes was then informed that he could not use boats of his own choice, which he had planned to purchase in Rangoon; the Burmese Government would provide boats and they would be accompanied by war boats for the protection of the party. There was no alternative but to agree; and no offence was taken by the Myowun when Symes insisted on employing a British shipwright from *Seahorse* to examine the boats selected.

They were not clear yet. The Myowun had consulted his astrologer and was advised that the propitious date for sailing was 28th May. Symes' party could not be ready by then and the Myowun, regretting the super-natural necessity of preceding his guests, departed on the given date with his own barge and the war-boats, having arranged to await the British party at Donabyu, some 100 miles up river.

Two days after the departure of the Myowun, Captain Michael Symes led his Embassy out from Rangoon on the long journey to Amarapoora. It was to take forty-seven days, but as close on half of these were spent in stops ashore, such a passage can be considered a remarkable performance for the heavy, elaborate type of boats used by the Mission and for the season of the year when the Irrawaddy would be rising strongly. Nature, however, has provided that in the peak months of the high water season from June to September the south-west monsoon wind blows with its full force to fill the sails of those travelling northwards up the river. So Symes' little fleet made good passage.

Captain Symes had been allotted a boat to himself, as were both his British colleagues. There was a kitchen boat, a baggage boat and two more for his Indian escort. The boats, sometimes described as barges when in royal colours or in use by high officials, were sixty feet in length with beam of twelve feet at widest, narrowing at both bow and stern. Built of teak with outriggers on both sides they could be rowed, poled or sailed. The crew of twenty-six not only worked but lived on stages built on the outriggers, protected from sun or rain by bamboo matting shelters. The captain took the helm and sat on a stage on the lofty stern; with him lay the decisions as to whether the boat would be rowed, poled or sailed and a fine judgement he exercised when both wind and current were strong. He may use his sail or put his boat close to the bank and allow his men to pole to make the best headway, or find slack water in which to use the oars. In short, his options were his art and much of it can still be seen on the Irrawaddy today. Rowing is rare, but sail is much in use and the art of poling is not lost; the outrigger stages are used as walkways, the top of the pole is placed at the collar bone and the men traverse the length of the boat from stem to stern following each other in quick succession.

Symes was in good spirits at the start of his journey up river. Despite the frustrations of the long delay awaiting the Royal approval for his departure from Rangoon he had liked the Burmese officials whom he had met and had judged that the liking was mutual. This affinity was to become an important factor in his Mission and in prolonging peaceful relationships between Britain and Burma in the years to follow, but in the meantime he did not realise that further frustrations awaited him at the Court of Ava and the indignities which he would have to suffer. He was determined to make a success of his Embassy and to understand the Burmese character and their ways strange to the European.

On that first day, with the great golden Shwe Dagon Pagoda gradually fading into the distance behind them, the seven boats used the flood tide to the fullest possible extent, rowing until three o'clock in the afternoon and then awaiting the next flood tide some seven hours later. By daybreak the next day they had covered seventy miles from Rangoon and were approaching the main Irrawaddy River. So far they had used the tidal Panhlaing Creek which flows from the Irrawaddy eastwards into the Rangoon River.

At the junction of the Irrawaddy and the Panhlaing Creek stands the town of Yandoon, already at that time a growing community and soon to become an important riverine trading centre. Here there is little influence from the tides of the sea and once in the main river the boats set their sails to the strong south-west wind that was now blowing. Without the tide to help them, however, progress was slow and it was two days later before they joined the Myowun thirty miles on at Donabyu. There they found a huge fleet of boats awaiting them.

With his barge and entourage, his war-boats and others who had joined the convoy for the protection it afforded, some one hundred boats of numerous shapes and sizes were assembled. This great fleet, led by the Myowun and the British party, moved off the next day, stretched out over several miles of river. When they reached Henzada, apex of the delta, on 4th June they had come through two days of continuous monsoon rain and the temperature had dropped to 78°F., no less than 20° below the torrid, still heat of Rangoon a week before.

The cooler air did nothing to reduce the humidity, which reaches unpleasantly high levels during the monsoon months in Lower Burma. On the river it has a particularly disagreeable quality, clothes and bedding being constantly moist and the lighting of lamps at nightfall bringing clouds of flying insects. The only refuge then is darkness — and mosquitoes! And when the rain has stopped, the wind will drop and a stillness will descend, bringing equally unwelcome heat to the humidity. The inevitable fevers follow, but in his journal Symes makes little reference to the health of his party or to the discomforts of the monsoon. He shows more concern for the boat crews, who were required to row or pole when the wind failed them, or sometimes to use a fourth means of forward movement by the men tracking in line with ropes along the bank pulling their boats in slack water.

A fair wind favoured the convoy leaving Henzada and took them over 100 miles to Prome in six days. The huge fleet sailing before the wind presented a spectacle rarely seen by the riverine population even in this district of watermen and boatbuilders. Numerous boats alongside the bank at every village were loading paddy (rice in the husk) grown in the area and being boated for areas of shortage in the dry zone further north. As the convoy approached the town of Prome, the mountains known as the Arakan Yomas loomed up far to the west behind the wide flat paddy growing plain. Here to the east the Pegu Yomas gradually close in towards the river and the proximity of these two mountain ranges at Prome, where they are only some forty miles apart, has determined the strategic position of this historic town, scene of many sieges and conflicts.

They were in forest country now, much of it teak. This remarkable hardwood, found only in Burma and adjacent Siam (Thailand), has provided over the ages the ideal timber for boat-building in a land where transport is largely water-borne. Already it was obvious to Symes that the Irrawaddy was the lifeline of Burma and that he was seeing boatbuilding on a scale required to sustain the natural trade of the country.

Three more days brought them to Myede (pronounced Myayday), then an important village but long since faded into obscurity, where the Myowun required a few days' stay to attend to his affairs, as this was the northern extremity of his Pegu Estates. So his entourage and the British party were transferred to bamboo houses ashore, where they remained for the next fourteen days. The stay was prolonged, as the convoy had to await a Royal escort to be sent down from Amarapoora before the Myowun could proceed with his British guests.

Headed by high Government officials, the escort duly arrived on 29th June and taking up the lead, joined the last stage in the long journey. Two days later, with sails filled by the strong south-west wind they were well into the central dry zone and made another stop at Yenangyaung, Burma's oil town.

Here, within a radius of a few miles from the river, an oil

industry had been established long past with successive generations of twenty-four families closely and jealously guarding their control of the wells. The oil was extracted manually, sometimes at depths of 300 feet, stored in earthenware jars and distributed both north and south by boats. It was used throughout the country for lamps, as a preservative on timber and for medicinal purposes.

To Symes it was something entirely new and drew from him expressions of amazement, to the delight of his hosts. Tactfully, he withheld any comment on the barren, arid countryside on which the wells were situated and the unpleasant odour of the oil which permeated the whole area.

While the people stared at Symes during these stops ashore, never having seen a British officer in uniform before, he has written that he was "much taken by their kindly attitude to strangers". Symes' own attitude to the Burmese people obviously drew a ready response. If he had a fault as the Governor-General's Emissary it was his readiness to gloss over events to come which could have humiliated and angered others, but this was his judgement in handling his task. He was to be confronted, as were other British Emissaries, with the contrasting attitudes on the one hand of the Ava Court and on the other of the ordinary people.

It took a week against the strong July river to reach Nyaungoo, where there was another shore excursion to see the pagodas of Pagan, ancient capital of an earlier dynasty. They remained there until on 11th July the royal barge arrived from Amarapoora and was placed at Symes' disposal. With sail and sixteen rowers on each side this was the finest barge on the river, with red painted hull, gilded superstructure and silken awnings; its presence and the courtesy it demonstrated to Captain Symes and his Embassy seemed to augur well.

It took another week to reach Amarapoora from Nyaungoo. This was fair progress in the month of July with at least 130 miles to cover. That is the measured distance, but the need to seek slack water required frequent crossings of the river, which even here, six hundred miles from the sea, is from three to four miles wide in the high water months.

Before pulling in at Amarapoora, then the capital, a ceremonial call was made at the old capital of Ava, only a few miles below Amarapoora, whither King Bodawpaya had moved his Court in 1782. The name Ava, however, continued to be used for the King's Court and was in fact to become the capital again in 1819, only to be replaced once more by Amarapoora in 1837. Superstition and ill-omens are the reasons recorded by history for these frequent moves, but there may be some truth in another reason — a simple matter of hygiene.

The British Envoy and his party, having arrived in Amarapoora on 17th July, were to wait the King's pleasure until the end of September and were unable to depart on their down-river journey until 25th October. Symes blamed these delays on French efforts to discredit him by spreading false rumours, carried to Rangoon by a French ship, of impending disasters to the British in India and of British military defeats in Europe. He was to experience these months of delay, for which this French 'news' was blamed, administered with the greatest outward courtesy but real humiliation of his Embassy; he drew the comparison of "the kindness to his private person and indignities to his public position". To his written entreaties for audience with the King, he received replies shrouded in veils of ambiguity.

But at last he was admitted to the Golden Feet (the King's presence) with his British aides, was observed for a few minutes and without a word being said found that the 'interview' was at an end. However, before permission was given for his departure he was to receive the royal reply to the message of friendship from the Governor-General. This contained a satisfactory assurance that British merchants should be allowed to trade in the Burmese Empire and that a Resident may reside at Rangoon "to superintend mercantile affairs and maintain a friendly intercourse". The Arakan-Chittagong frontier incidents were forgotten for the time being, but were far from over.

As his boats pulled out from the foreshore at Amarapoora, Captain Symes must undoubtedly have felt a quiet satisfaction at the success, however limited, of his Mission, despite those weary frustrating months. He had carried out his duty in a manner which he believed served the best interests of his country and as a long-serving soldier of still modest rank he may have allowed himself a thought to the possibility of some advancement in the Service for himself. In this he was not to be disappointed.

After an uneventful passage down river the party reached Rangoon on 17th November, rejoined *Seahorse* and were back in Calcutta before Christmas.

CHAPTER TWO

SETTING THE SCENE

I. The River

The Irrawaddy has its source at the confluence of two rivers, the Mali Hka and the N'mai Hka, both of which find their beginnings in the Himalayan massif. In the same watershed the sources of three other great rivers are to be found; the Salween, which debouches like the Irrawaddy into the Bay of Bengal; and the Mekong and Yangtse Kiang, which flow into the South China Sea.

The volume of water contributed to these and other rivers by that vast mountainous area of China and Tibet is beyond calculable dimensions. The melting snow from these Himalayan peaks brings about the phenomenon that the Irrawaddy, which flows from north to south in Burma, begins its early annual rise during the month of April in the heart of Burma's driest season. From year to year the snow-line of the peaks varies and on this depends the timing and volume of water which descends into the valleys. The arrival of hot southerly winds in March or April to melt the snows also provides a variable factor, so that only by careful observation of the river level at the northern towns of Myitkyina and Bhamo can warning of the advent of the first rise in the Irrawaddy be given.

The rains of the south-west monsoon seldom reach Lower Burma until mid-May or Upper Burma until June. When they add their volume of water to the already swollen river, the season of high water becomes fully established and persists until the month of October. In the northern catchment area of the Irrawaddy average rainfall during the south-west monsoon months of April to October is 80 inches, in the central dry zone only 25 to 45 inches and in the delta area 100 inches or more. From November until March the dry north-east monsoon covers the whole country.

The river begins to fall in October and reaches its lowest levels between December and April. During this low water season the level will drop 80 to 100 feet in the First Defile below

Myitkyina, while over the 750 miles between Bhamo and Henzada the drop is on average about 40 feet. At Henzada, 150 miles from the sea (where the Irrawaddy is four miles wide) the first branches of the delta break out east and west and from there south the whole country is flat and alluvial, with no defined or measurable rise and fall of the river.

The Irrawaddy has an exceptionally small contour drop of only some 500 feet in the 1100 miles from the confluence of the two rivers to the sea. Yet the current speed is maintained even during the low water season, often at modest levels where the river widens, but at greater velocity where a narrowing of the natural banks occurs.

With huge sediment deposits suspended by the current, silt and sand dictate the nature of the river bed. The sand is of the finest texture and almost white in colour, but where the river is subject to the tidal influence of the delta area it can only be described as muddy, and seasonal flooding there accounts for the remarkable fertility of the delta paddy growing land. The quantity of alluvial deposit is so immense that the delta extends further and further into the Bay of Bengal each year; geological evidence has shown that the town of Prome, now some 250 miles from the sea, was once close to the seaboard.

In this delta area a low water season of defined creeks is transformed by high water into many vast, lake-like surfaces. Below Henzada the ever increasing branches which form the delta spread east and west until, finally, across a land space of more than one hundred miles between the Bassein River to the west and the Rangoon River to the east, the Irrawaddy pours out its muddy waters over a wide expanse of the ocean.

2. Eighteenth Century Burma

Burma attracted scant attention from the rest of the world before the nineteenth century. Nor did she invite it. Left on their own the Burmese are a self-contained people; nature, having amply endowed them with the resources of their land and rivers to sustain their physical welfare, also provides them with a philosophy of contentment, founded on family and their Buddhist faith.

It would be wrong, however, to say that Burma went completely unnoticed. As far back as 1435 a Venetian merchant named Nicolo di Conti was known to have been trading in the country and in 1519 the Portuguese established a small trading post at Martaban, on the estuary of the Salween River; this was part of the wide exploitation by the Portuguese of Vasco de Gama's discovery of the Cape of Good Hope route to the Indies.

The first Englishman to set foot in Burma was Ralph Fitch, a notable merchant adventurer of his time. Having found his way out to India by land he took passage in 1586 on a Portuguese vessel from Serampore to Negrais, thence to Bassein and through the delta of the Irrawaddy to the new Portuguese settlement at Syriam, near to Pegu. Fitch later became a Director of the Levant Company and was a leading figure in the formation of the East India Company, which received its Royal Charter in 1600.

In the seventeenth century trading posts, which became known as factories, were established by the Dutch, British and French East India Companies on the Burma coast, the British, and later the French, favouring Syriam for its position on the wide eastern estuary of the Irrawaddy delta. When the Burmese Government would not allow the export of teak the British began to build teak ships in 1720 at Syriam and soon the French followed suit; thus, and only thus would the Burmese agree that teak could leave their shores.

This was the extent of European involvement when in the eighteenth century the Burmese King Alaungpaya sought expansion of his kingdom by force of arms. Within the Burma that we know today there was division, the Mons who occupied the southern part of the country retaining their individuality, if not always their territorial independence, in the face of incursions by the Burmese which dispossessed them of their land. In 1752, having taken advantage of distractions created by raids from northern enemies on the Burmese Kingdom of Ava, the Mons seized their own southern territory, which was then under Burmese subjugation, and proceeded to over-run practically the whole country including the capital city, also named Ava. They deposed the Burmese King and were well on the way to revenging fully past defeats when they were stopped in their triumphant tracks at Shwebo, a small town now but then little more than a village, which lies between the valleys of the Chindwin and Irrawaddy Rivers. The local thugyi (headman) there put up a successful resistance, went on to establish a Burmese national movement and drove the Mons from Upper

Burma. He was raised to the throne of Burma as King Alaung-paya and re-established the Court of Ava.

The new King had reconquered the Lower Burma of the Mons by 1757 and founded the city of Rangoon, deciding that this was to be the main port for his Kingdom. Until then all that was there was the small fishing village of Dagon, famous for the magnificent Shwe Dagon Pagoda which had already been a sacred place for many centuries of Buddhist pilgrimage. Alaungpaya then destroyed the nearby Mon port of Syriam and this immediately involved both British and French interests.

In this strategically well-placed haven for the Bay of Bengal British and French East India Companies built their ships and lived in apparent harmony, but naval rivalry for command of the Indian Ocean led to attempts by each to oust the other. The French, however, had alienated Burmese opinion by supporting the Mons in their efforts against the Burmese invasion, while the British had established a garrison at Cape Negrais at the mouth of the Bassein River. This move led to a close British relationship with King Alaungpaya, as Negrais became . an arsenal from where the King was supplied with military equipment. But the friendly relationship was shortlived and the outcome of many misunderstandings was a massacre of the British garrison by the King's forces. Attempts to conciliate and re-establish trade and ship-building were abortive and with the French threat removed, British interest waned. All relations between the Court of Ava and the British East India Company, who ruled India, therefore ceased completely. It was by then 1762.

Between 1762 and 1794 there was an apparently deliberate policy of the East India Company to ignore Burma. Events on the Arakan frontier in 1794 affecting the Chittagong district of Bengal, however, caused the Company's Governor-General in Calcutta to write to the Court of Ava in an attempt to clear up differences which had arisen between them. The Arakanese, always an unwillingly subjugated people, had rebelled against their Burmese masters and taken refuge in the adjoining Chittagong district when hard pressed. This led to accusations of harbouring the rebels and aroused the East India Company's Government to the realisation that communication with Burma on the Arakan frontier issue was necessary.

King Alaungpaya had died in 1760 and was followed on the throne by three of his sons in succession, the second and third being of a similar warlike character to their father. Siam was over-run by the second and only saved from complete defeat by Chinese intervention, which eventually enabled the Siamese to drive out the Burmese invaders. It was the third and ablest of the sons, Bodawpaya (1782-1819) who conquered Arakan and subjected his enlarged Kingdom to an era of conscription, not only for warlike purposes, but for restoration of public works and to satisfy the Burmese obsession for the building of pagodas. His massive Mingun pagoda, uncompleted and split by earthquake, still stands on the west bank of the Irrawaddy a few miles above Amarapoora, where he had built his new capital. Throughout the land he was employing thousands of Mons, Shans and Arakanese as forced labour.

It was from this oppression that the Arakanese had rebelled in 1794 and brought about renewed British interest in Burma. By early 1795 the situation was so tense that the Governor-General, having received no satisfactory response to his letter, had decided to send an Envoy to the Court of Ava. Hence the historic river journey of Captain Michael Symes.

CHAPTER THREE

BRITISH RESIDENTS

I. Hiram Cox

There is a township called Cox's Bazaar in the Chittagong District of Bangladesh, the new Republic which until recently was East Pakistan, and before partition in 1947 was East Bengal in the continent of British India. The problems of over-population and famine which beset Bangladesh today were less evident in the eighteenth century in Bengal, but Chittagong has always been a poverty-stricken area, subject to all too frequent floods from the monsoon rains.

Arakan, the adjacent region to the south in Burma, is more fortunate in its topography, with the Arakan Yoma Hill Tracts ranging the whole of its length on the east and a succession of rivers flowing from the hills into the Bay of Bengal. The western plain is alluvial, producing abundant paddy crops. The Arakanese, however, have been less fortunate in other ways. Although akin, they are quite a separate people to the Burmese and their territory was in their own independent hands until they were overrun by an aggressive Burmese King in the eleventh century. Recapturing their independence in the thirteenth century, they were able to repel frequent attempts to subjugate them, until in 1785 King Bodawpaya of Burma included Arakan in his conquests. It remained a Province of the Burmese Empire until ceded to Britain in 1826.

In our own time, Arakan became a battle-field from 1942 to 1945 in the war with the Japanese. With access mainly through the port of Chittagong and the South Chittagong District, the whole coastline and hinterland became familiar ground to many thousands of British Service men and women, many of whom will at one time or other have seen Cox's Bazaar. They will recall that the inhabitants in the township and surrounding area dressed mostly in the colourful Burmese way, to which the Arakanese style is identical; these were the descendants of the unfortunate people who fled 150 years before from Burmese oppression in Arakan.

30

Hiram Cox, who gave his name to the settlement, established there in 1799 a colony of refugees from the nearby Arakan Hill Tracts. He left not only his name but also his mark, for the success of his work was outstanding. But the beginning of his short diplomatic career, three years earlier, was not quite so successful.

In 1796 Cox was selected by the Governor-General of India to be British Resident at Rangoon, the appointment approved by King Bodawpaya in his reply given to Captain Symes the previous year. Cox was a soldier of the Indian Service, being a Lieutenant in the 3rd Bengal European Regiment when selected. As he was then thirty-six years of age some surprise may reasonably be expressed that this unknown officer of modest rank should suddenly be noticed for a diplomatic post in a notoriously sensitive and complex country.

But noticed he was and promoted to Captain before departing for Rangoon in September 1796. Judging by most historical records, it would not be over-stating the case to say that he made a bad start and never looked back. Yet the criticisms he made of Symes' Mission were accepted by some when he returned to Calcutta; and he brought intelligence of aggressive Burmese intentions towards Assam and Chittagong which proved well founded. Otherwise his residency at Rangoon was something of a non-event and he spent almost a year of his time in Burma getting himself up to Amarapoora, going through the process of the eternal wait to see the King and returning to Rangoon.

His river journeys from Rangoon to Amarapoora and back therefore became an important part of the eighteen months which Captain Hiram Cox spent in Burma. He kept a journal, but his premature death in Chittagong the year after he returned from his Rangoon Residency robbed him of the opportunity of giving his own account. His son, however, told the story in 1821 by publishing a book in which he presented the journal and defended his father's record against the critics. But the facts seem to point to a different conclusion. A successful Envoy to Burma, indeed any success in Burma for a foreigner, requires a very large measure of patience with and understanding of the Burmese way of life, mind and behaviour. Cox does not seem to have possessed or acquired any of these.

Yet in the extraordinary and unpredictable way in which the Burmese Kings would act, Cox succeeded in obtaining the

Royal permission to proceed to the Court of Ava with an unusual promptness. He had wasted no time in falling-out with Burmese officials in Rangoon, mainly over his status, and it was on this account that he had requested permission to go to Amarapoora in the hope that he would be accorded the recognition that he believed he was due.

There is little doubt that he was the victim of circumstances. British weakness over the Arakan refugee problem gave the Burmese a false impression of the power of the Raj and led them to adopt a truculent attitude to British approaches. Also, his instructions from the Governor-General gave Cox a mistaken idea that his appointment carried a higher standing than was ever envisaged in the Burmese King's message. He did, however, add to his problems by the manner of his insistence on his status and by his stubborn attitude to Burmese procedure.

The Myowun of Pegu comes on the scene again, as does one Baba Sheen, an Armenian by extraction who held the important post of Collector of Taxes in Rangoon. The latter first appeared accompanying the Myowun and Symes the previous year as interpreter and was again assigned with the Myowun to Cox. And more British Envoys were to learn, as both Symes and Cox did, to distrust this "high officer of business skill and general knowledge" to quote Symes. But he was indispensible to them, and Cox had to appear to trust him, while all the time he knew him to be the chief cause of the failure of his Mission.

It was Baba Sheen, the wolf in sheep's clothing so to speak, for he dressed in the Burmese style, who aroused the greatest resentment in Cox by his high-handed and devious actions; the Armenian had the simple objective of ensuring that the British did not gain favour at the Ava Court. And this resentment Cox was unable to conceal, for he took it as an affront not only to himself but also to his country. The Myowun was kindly and frequently offered advice to Cox, but to no avail.

So, with this unpropitious background of circumstances, we turn our attention to the journey on the Irrawaddy which Captain Hiram Cox made from Rangoon to Amarapoora in his endeavour to secure from King Bodawpaya recognition in the high capacity which he demanded, and which he was refused in Rangoon. No other purpose for this long journey is recorded, by Cox himself or elsewhere, yet it does seem likely that he had instructions to find a reason for visiting the Burmese capital. However, one would hardly think that the reason he chose was one which the Governor-General would have had in mind.

The account which Cox left of this river journey shows that it followed much of the pattern as recorded by Symes, except that significantly there is no reference to an escort of any kind or of any ceremonial meetings such as were accorded to Symes.

Captain Cox had arrived in Rangoon on 10th October, 1796, by the East India Company's packet *Swallow,* an event which he apparently celebrated by immediately coming to cross purposes with the Shabunder (Master Attendant of the Port) over the regulations to be observed by foreign ships while in port. He seems to have made little endeavour to settle down to a Residency in Rangoon and soon he was seeking permission to see the King. Unpredictably, by mid-November orders came back from Amarapoora to the Pegu Myowun for boats to be prepared and the British Resident in Rangoon duly embarked with his one Assistant and the usual retinue of servants on 5th December.

Navigation of the Irrawaddy in the months of December and January presents problems quite different from those encountered by the Symes' party in June and July. The river is low in December and lower in January and the south-west monsoon has given way to the light north-east monsoon which brings dry and cooler weather. Thus the use of sail would only be possible where wide stretches permitted a tacking course to be set and generally rowing and poling would be the order of the day.

The force of current is reduced greatly to the advantage of the rowers, but the inability to set sails, and the lengthy winding course to be taken when the water is low, militate against the low water season passage. Cox took eighteen days to reach Prome, compared with twelve days taken by Symes in June the previous year; only by spending less time in stops ashore en route he reached Amarapoora in fifty-five days. Symes had taken forty-seven.

The comfort of these early British travellers on the Irrawaddy was an important reason for the length of time taken for their journeys. A war-boat carrying despatches, and with a crew of rowers numbering up to forty, could make the passage from Rangoon to Amarapoora in ten days in the high water season, and the return down river in no more than four days. In the low water season they could make the same up passage in eight days and come down in six. But the war-boats were of light canoe type construction with no space for any comfort and the rowers were subject to constant physical strain.

The log which Cox wrote of his river journey is couched in quite different terms from the Symes' journal of the previous year. Symes was transparently full of enthusiasm and the excitement of his task, while it is not difficult to detect in Cox a determination to put right the wrong which he saw in the stubborn refusal of Rangoon officialdom to understand that he was an important Envoy of the Governor-General. His expectations were unfulfilled and he brooded during his weeks on the river. Yet he had the advantage over Symes that he was travelling in the cold weather season, when the weather is dry and fine, day in day out. The fascination of the river is immeasurably increased in this season compared with the south-west monsoon period and personal comfort is also greatly enhanced.

The only account of his shore excursions worthy of note is that of several days stay at Yenangyaung, where he made a detailed study of the oilwells and some estimates of production. No doubt a full report on the extraordinary oilwells of Burma was prepared by Captain Cox for the Governor-General's Council in Calcutta.

Cox's little party arrived at Amarapoora on 24th January, 1797. We shall not dwell too long on his wait of nine months at the Court of Ava or on how he made life more and more difficult for himself by his obstinacy. He was received by the King in audience and was promised that his status would be given proper consideration, but although this promise was repeated nothing happened. Yet after the relatively short time of two months he might have been wise to have accepted that he had made his point and left it at that. The Myowun of Pegu was then returning down river and pressed Cox to accompany him, assuring him that the Royal Order for his proper recognition would be brought down by messenger in due course. Cox rejected this good advice and while one can sympathise with his scepticism, the account of his frustrations thereafter makes sorry reading.

Finally on 17th October he applied for royal permission to leave the capital and, receiving no reply, hired his own boats and proceeded down river. Thirteen days later when he arrived in Rangoon he found that a Royal Order awaited him commanding his return to Amarapoora.

Determined to evade any such thing, Cox sent a message to Calcutta asking for the despatch of a frigate to rescue him. He enlisted support from local British merchants and, with trade threatened, Rangoon officials quietly allowed nothing to happen until in due course Cox was formally recalled to Calcutta. At the same time letters were despatched by the Governor-General to King Bodawpaya and to the Myowun, announcing Cox's recall and requesting them to assist him in his early departure. Cox himself was advised of these despatches, which were calculated "to preclude the necessity of sending a vessel of force" to take him out of Burma. The letter to the King was couched in apologetic language and included the proposal that "another gentleman in whom we have the greatest confidence will be sent to reside in Rangoon".

As soon as Cox began to prepare for departure, he received the Myowun's invitation to stay as his guest for the approaching water festival of Thadingyut. Then when he went aboard the frigate *Carolina,* which had been sent to fetch him back to India, he received a thirteen gun salute from the Burmese shore batteries; and yet another conciliatory move was the arrival of a royal war-boat alongside before he sailed with a message from the King advising him of an order to "grant to Captain Hiram Cox ground for his house and garden at Rangoon wherever he chooses, etc.". It was too late, Cox was on his way. The Governor-General never received a reply to the proposal to send another gentleman to Rangoon.

While Cox was in Burma another serious Arakan frontier incident occurred, resulting in thousands of Arakanese crossing the border into Chittagong. This exodus culminated in some 40,000 people from the Arakan side settling in south Chittagong District and the British authorities in India had to undertake large-scale relief measures. It was to this area that Captain Cox was sent as soon as he arrived back from Rangoon early in 1798 to supervise the relief and settle the unfortunate Arakanese, and here that he died the following year at the early age of 39. But in that short time he had established his township and left his name in the annals of British Indian history.

It was not until 1802 that the Governor-General of India, then Lord Wellesley, could be persuaded to send another Envoy to the Court of Ava. Wellesley had arrived in India in 1798 at a critical time and was immediately surrounded by problems within the Presidencies which precluded much thought for Burma. The experiences of Symes and Cox also were hardly conducive to any hope of establishing good relations with this wayward neighbour. But at last he agreed that contact should be restored and decided that the best man to do this was Michael Symes, by then a Lieutenant-Colonel. His Embassy can only be described as abortive; nothing was achieved beyond friendly exchanges and these only by the exercise of the great patience with which Symes was amply endowed. This was all the more remarkable with Baba Sheen again appointed as the main link with the Burmese King; even he came under the spell of Symes' diplomatic skill. The Envoy was again impressed by the ordinary Burmese people who, he wrote

"are from nature kind and benevolent but the miserable system of their government perverts their native disposition."

Three further Embassies were sent to the Burmese capital between 1803 and 1813, all led by Captain John Canning of the Bengal Native Infantry, who had accompanied Symes in 1802 and was selected by him. While helping to maintain peace these efforts to reach an understanding, particularly on the Arakan frontier problem, met with little success.

2. John Crawfurd

The East India Company were alarmed in 1817 when Burma invaded and conquered Assam. Added to the uncertainties of Arakan, they believed that all Indian frontiers with Burma were now threatened and that invasion was not only possible, but likely.

King Bodawpaya's grandson, Bagyidaw, succeeded to the throne of Burma in 1819 and with his aggressive and brilliant general, Maha Bandoola, began to prepare for offensives against Bengal. The Calcutta Government moved first, however. The result was the First Burmese War of 1824-26 in which a large British and Indian force was despatched to Burma and which ended after they had arrived at Yandabo, only fifty miles from Ava, once again the Burmese capital. Rangoon had been taken, also the whole of Lower and Central Burma, but the Treaty of Yandabo demanded and secured only the cession of Arakan, Assam, Manipur and Tenasserim. Bandoola had been killed in an epic battle at Donabyu on the Irrawaddy, leaving his name to posterity in Burma as a national hero.

British relations with Burma should now have been more strongly founded, the Treaty providing that a British Resident should be properly received at the Court of Ava and negotiations opened for a separate treaty of commerce. This was in February 1826, but it was not until October that John Crawfurd arrived in Ava as British Resident. The Burmese had by that time recovered from the shock of defeat and loss of their conquered territories and Crawfurd was confronted with the usual frustrating tactics which completely thwarted his attempts to conclude a satisfactory commercial treaty. He remained in Ava only until December, when he left in despair and advised Calcutta that there was little purpose in posting a permanent Resident at the Ava Court. Preoccupation with problems in India prevented the Governor-General from doing other than accepting Crawfurd's advice, at least for the time being.

Crawfurd, however, left a scholarly record of his river journeys, which were momentous if for no other reason than that they heralded the arrival of the steam engine in Burma. But there was much more to them than that.

John Crawfurd was born on the island of Islay, for all his Ayrshire name. He took a degree in medicine at Edinburgh, serving thereafter in the Army as a doctor in India, Penang and Java. He became a distinguished Orientalist, so much so that he was sent as an Envoy to Siam and then succeeded Stamford Raffles in Singapore. His appointment to Ava, therefore, points to the importance attached to the Residency there at that particular time. The Burmese rebuff even to this eminent Envoy demonstrated, above all, their reluctance to accept the "insult" that his credentials came from the Governor-General of India and not from the Sovereign in London. Throughout this long period of unsatisfactory relations between the two countries, this constantly rankled with the Burmese and was a major cause of diplomatic failures.

Crawfurd had at his disposal "the first steam vessel ever in India", to quote the official record, which had been sent over to Burma for the war and was retained for special duty. *Diana* was a small paddler of 130 tons burthen, built of teak at Kidderpore Dockyard, Calcutta, and belonging to the Bengal Marine. She appears to have achieved a top speed of about six knots, adequate for the Irrawaddy low water season but liable to go in the wrong direction while at full speed ahead against a strong high water flood. Yet think of the excitement and wonder this new invention must have created on the river and the "awe-za" (a Burmese word which means something more than standing and respect) for its occupants. *Diana* with her long funnel had presented such an awesome spectacle to General Bandoola's soldiers as she steamed up to Donabyu for that last battle, with paddles threshing furiously and smoke and flames belching from her funnel, that many ran in terror.

There was only one *Diana,* however, and the Envoy's large party required to be accommodated mainly in the usual country boats. He had an impressive escort commanded by a British Officer with twenty-eight British Grenadiers of H.M. 87th Regiment and fifteen Indian Sepoy Grenadiers. He was accompanied by Dr Wallick, Superintendent of the Botanical Gardens of Calcutta, who had been sent to report on the resources of the forests of Pegu and Ava, as well as those in the recently acquired possessions south of the Salween River in Tenasserim. The American missionary Adoniram Judson was in the party also, as interpreter. Dr. Judson had by this time achieved fame by his remarkable Christian conversions to the American Baptist Mission amongst the Karen peoples of Burma.

Diana took Crawfurd to Ava in twenty-nine days, departing from Rangoon on 2nd September. He reckoned she could have made that September passage in about twenty days but for the frequent towing of boats of his convoy which were lagging behind. As was customary with early steamships, *Diana* was rigged with masts on which sail would be set to add to her propulsion and the south-west monsoon wind provided useful assistance to the passage.

There is an interesting comment in Crawfurd's Journal on Bengal coal, carried to fire the boiler in *Diana;* it was found that "old discarded teak" gave better results and some regret was expressed that it was not too readily available. There is also mention in the Journal of the Burmese delicacy, ngapi, likening it to the balachaung of the Malays. Ngapi is fish salted and dried in the sun to acquire sharp tasting qualities, and in the process it acquires high smelling qualities also. It is produced in the delta area where both the fish and salt are plentiful.

By the time Crawfurd came to make the downwards passage from Ava in December, the river was low and he experienced many groundings. At Pakokku, near the junction of the

38

Chindwin River and the Irrawaddy and some one hundred miles below Ava, he describes *Diana* dropping down a dangerous channel on a kedge anchor, a manoeuvre which in later years was frequently practised. At Sinbyugyun, letters from Calcutta were received, having been carried across the Arakan mountain range by runners; and from there Crawfurd despatched letters which reached Calcutta in twenty-five days. Then after leaving Yenangyaung *Diana* took the ground badly. That was on 27th December, and she was refloated only on 3rd January by lightening her and with the help of no less than 300 Burmese heaving her off her sandbank. The lightening included sawing off one third of the poop.

With these delays it actually took Crawfurd longer to come down river than to go up. He spent only a few days in Rangoon before departing in the *Diana* for Moulmein, the Tenasserim headquarters of the British occupation forces at the mouth of the Salween River.

From there, late in January 1827, he made a five days journey by *Diana* on the Ataran River, which rises to the south-east in Siam and flows in a north-west direction through Tenasserim into the estuary of the Salween and Gyaing Rivers. The Salween, one of the great rivers of Burma, which forms much of her frontier with China, would seem to have been more deserving of that first steamer, but the Ataran in Crawfurd's words is "the deepest although the smallest of the three rivers". The Salween is navigable for only fifty-five miles, owing to rapids, and the Gyaing for forty-two and then only when the tides serve.

The purpose of this short expedition on the Ataran River was to enable Dr. Wallick to see teak forests prospected a few months earlier by an adventurous British official who travelled by land some 100 miles to the Siamese frontier, reaching a place called Three Pagodas (later to give its name to Three Pagodas Pass on the infamous Japanese death railway of 1942-45) and finding two large teak forests close to the Ataran. Crawfurd was able to confirm the practicability of bringing the teak when felled to the river, from where it could be rafted down to Moulmein; these became the first British teak forests to be leased for commercial extraction. The first sawmills were built in Moulmein as a result.

Some idea of the economic prospect which this held out for Tenasserim can be gained from the size of these forests and of the teak trees growing there. Over an area of some twenty square miles there were trees standing up to sixty feet in height, the largest with a girth at their base of fifteen feet.

Animal life abounded, elephant especially; wild pig, the most dangerous of all Burma jungle beasts; monkeys who inhabited the precipitous high banks of the river; and the small deer common to all Burma forests. The birds were spectacular, numerous pea-fowl, jungle fowl with equally brilliant plumage, the large green pigeon and other smaller birds of the forest. So sparsely inhabited was the whole area that much of this jungle life had rarely been disturbed by man.

Returning to Moulmein, which was then mainly a military station under the command of General Sir Archibald Campbell, who had led the British force in the war, Crawfurd delayed only long enough to report on his journey. He sailed early in February for Calcutta, but left *Diana* in Burma, probably his greatest regret. He had achieved little for such a distinguished Envoy and this at a time when progress with the Burmese seemed possible. He was the first, but not the last, British official to learn that a Treaty in Burma in these days was not quite so sacrosanct as their experience elsewhere had taught them to expect.

CHAPTER FOUR

A FLOTILLA FOR THE IRRAWADDY

Between Crawfurd's Mission in 1826/7 and the Second Burmese War in 1852 some limited success attended British efforts to maintain friendly relations with Burma. In 1830 Major Henry Burney, a military schoolmaster in Calcutta, was offered and accepted the appointment of British Resident at the Court of Ava, following agreement by King Bagyidaw to receive an Envoy from the Governor-General of India. Burney achieved a remarkable rapport with the King and, in the course of the seven years that he spent at the Ava Court, settled a dispute over the Manipur frontier which staved off further conflict between British India and Burma. But two years after he left in 1837 Tharrawaddy Min, who had deposed his brother Bagyidaw in a *coup d'etat,* made life impossible for a British Resident, relations deteriorated and Burney's successor was withdrawn.

The Second Burmese War began in April 1852 following many contraventions of the Yandabo Treaty, a series of incidents and finally an ultimatum ignored by the Ava Court. The three ports, Rangoon, Bassein and Martaban, were quickly taken by a British force from India before the monsoon rains began and in July the Governor-General of India, Lord Dalhousie, paid a visit to Rangoon to confer with the Army and Navy Commanders. He decided that the objective must go no further than annexation of the Province of Pegu, which would then link up Arakan and Tenasserim and result in the whole of lower Burma coming under British control. It would also result in isolating the King's Burma from her sea-ports and eliminate her as a potential danger to India.

To support this plan, which would involve maintaining a line of communication on the Irrawaddy between Rangoon and Thayetmyo, a distance of 300 miles, Dalhousie ordered a flotilla of river steamers and flats (shallow draft barges with covered decks) to be sent over to Rangoon from Calcutta. The Bengal Marine had established river flotillas on the Hooghly and

Brahmaputra for the transport and supply of troops and these included a type of paddle steamer which met the requirements for the Irrawaddy. They were side paddlers 125 feet in length with a light draught of two feet, powered by a single oscillating engine with two cylinders. This gave them a speed of $7\frac{1}{2}$ knots with one flat in tow, which was the limit of their towing capability.

Of the four paddlers detailed for Burma by the Bengal Marine, one had been built in 1832, two in 1833 and the fourth in 1838, all at Lambeth on the Thames. The *Lord William Bentinck* was steamed out to Calcutta in 1832, but this obviously remarkable feat of seamanship was not repeated when the *Damoodah* and *Nerbudda* were completed the following year, and the *Jumna* in 1838; the hulls of all three were dismantled, shipped out to Calcutta and re-erected there.

The flats which accompanied the four steamers to Rangoon were the hulls of even older steamers from which engines, boilers and upperworks had been removed, leaving clear decks which made spacious accommodation for troops. Permanent awnings from bow to stern provided protection from the sun and rain, and side awnings could be raised or lowered as required.

This flotilla of four paddlers and their flats made the crossing from Calcutta to Rangoon at the tail end of the south-west monsoon late in October, 1852. Weather conditions must have been carefully chosen and a fair measure of providence counted upon with a distance to cover in open sea of 800 miles from the mouth of the Hooghly to the Rangoon River. This could hardly have been accomplished in less than a week and October weather in the Bay of Bengal can be tempestuous.

The steamers were manned by British Officers of the Bengal Marine and lascar seamen from Chittagong, natural watermen of the rivers and creeks of Bengal, many of whose compatriots were already enlisted as country boat crews in Burma in support of the military operation. These in turn had their origin during the First Burmese War in 1824-26, when heavy mortality among boat crews of British sailors had prompted the Senior Naval Officer to apply for lascars to work the river craft. Seven hundred were sent over from Chittagong with three officers and Government instructions that "on no account were their officers to be removed as they understood the management of the men".

With the flotilla on station, preparations for the advance on Prome were then completed and carried out with little

42

opposition, Prome being occupied during November, 1852. The original plan had been to establish both the military cantonment and the frontier at Thayetmyo, forty miles above Prome and a sizeable village. But having taken Thayetmyo and confirmed its suitability as the northern cantonment station, it was decided that a more defensible frontier would be secured by extending the line to Myede, some seven miles upriver; and Myede was at the known and established frontier of the Pegu Province.

Lord Dalhousie had also decided that it would be futile to force the Burmese King to acknowledge the conquest of Pegu in a Treaty, although this had been the wish of the British Government in London. He resolved to announce annexation by proclamation and have no more useless treaties to create further dissension in the future. The proclamation was read in Rangoon on 20th December, 1852 and the announcement made that Major Phayre, then Commissioner of Arakan, was to be the Commissioner of the new Pegu Province.

Arthur Purves Phayre had become a cadet in the Bengal Army in 1828 at the age of sixteen. He served as a subaltern and later as Civil Assistant to the Commissioner in Tenasserim, spending many years of his early service in that Province and acquiring an intimate knowledge of civil administration and of the Burmese language. His appointment to be Commissioner of Arakan in 1849 was the first step in a long and distinguished career in Burma and now he was entrusted with Pegu and the additional responsibility of maintaining relations with the Court of Ava.

The British conquest and annexation of Pegu had precipitated another palace revolution in Amarapoora and in February, 1853, the Mindon Prince was placed on the throne, deposing his incompetent brother Pagan Min who had reigned for only seven years. Mindon Min was to reign for the next twenty-five years, and to bring a stability to the Court of Ava by his strong sense of public duty and desire for peaceful relations with the British in Lower Burma. This is not to say that he was weak; on the contrary, he was as strong a King as the Burmese had known since Alaungpaya and maintained a stubborn refusal to accept by treaty or formally in any way that Pegu was lost to his kingdom for ever. But he was aware of the power of his neighbours in British India and, being a realist, sought friendly relations with them.

Between Mindon Min and Phayre an understanding

developed over the next two years, due mainly to a remarkable man, Thomas Spears. Phayre was unable to make the journey to Amarapoora, preoccupied as he was with problems arising from the unsettled state of Pegu after the 1852 war, and Spears became his eyes and ears in Upper Burma.

Thomas Spears, a native of Kirkcaldy, had been trading in piecegoods and silk at Amarapoora since the capital returned there in 1837. He was jailed with other Europeans when the 1852 war started and was held for nine months until released by King Mindon. The new King immediately took a strong liking to him and began to consult him almost daily. When Spears visited Rangoon he met Phayre and the Commissioner recognised in him the very man for whom he was looking, an intelligence agent at Amarapoora. Spears was agreeable to undertake this assignment, provided he did not have to conceal from the King the fact that he was corresponding with the Commissioner; and when Mindon was told of the appointment he was more than pleased and made sure that Spears' reports to Rangoon included messages which he himself wished to convey to the British. Lord Dalhousie, whose approval was required for this somewhat bizarre arrangement, had agreed after he had met Spears during another visit to Burma, but made it clear to Phayre that Spears was to be given no official position and must simply be a news-writer. Whatever they called him, he became a valuable agent at the capital and the mutual trust between him and the King contributed in no small measure to the friendly relationship between Britain and Burma which developed and which was to last for twenty years and more.

With Pegu pacified, Lord Dalhousie decided in 1855 that a Mission should go to the Court of Ava and that Major Phayre should be its leader. Diplomatic relations were to be placed on a more formal footing and a commercial treaty negotiated to enable a greater exchange of trade to develop between British Lower Burma and the King's Upper Burma. The grandeur of the Raj was to be fully displayed, not only to the Court at Amarapoora but to the Burmese people on the river journey, and every opportunity taken to demonstrate that there was nothing despotic about British rule.

Two of the steamers of the Irrawaddy Flotilla were released from their commissariat duties between Rangoon and Thayetmyo and suitably fitted out for the Mission. The *Lord William Bentinck* and the *Nerbudda,* when ready for the large party detailed by the Commissioner, were an impressive sight each with their flat in tow alongside and British flags and ensigns at their mastheads. The entourage of the Envoy was equally impressive, with twelve army and naval officers of the Lower Burma garrisons forming his suite and an Indian Officer with fifteen men of the 8th Cavalry, complete with their mounts, providing the escort. The Superintendent of the Geological Survey of India, a surgeon, an interpreter and the artist Colesworthy Grant completed the party.

No detail has been given of the early part of the river journey in an account written by the Secretary to the Mission, Captain (later Sir) Henry Yule, except to say that they set off from Rangoon on 1st August, 1855. Having stopped at Thayetmyo, where they embarked part of the band of the 29th Regiment, they left Myede on the 11th and crossed the frontier into Upper Burma. On the same day they were met by a Court deputation with six war boats to escort them in the King's territory. A more formal and larger reception was to take place at Pagan and a third close to the capital at Kyauktalon.

Remembering that August is the height of the high water season of the Irrawaddy, the slow rate of progress of the paddlers towing their flats is not surprising. They were obviously making poor way against the strong current in the relatively narrow river, less than half a mile wide in parts, between the frontier and Minhla, for they covered only forty miles in two days. But after Minhla, as the river widens out in the great central Burma plain, the current slackens and the daily run improved.

The twin towns, Minbu on the west bank and Magwe on the east bank, where they arrived on 13th August, marked the first large population centres in the King's Burma. The short run of some 25 miles from Magwe to Yenangyaung took eight hours and there three days were spent, in Yule's words, "inspecting the workings of the oil business and the barren scene with the coal-tarry odour of the petroleum".

The steamers of the Mission met a rising river after leaving the oilfields, but the spread of water over the wide Irrawaddy at this part of its course — from Yenangyaung to the Chindwin River mouth it is from three to four miles in width — reduced the current sufficiently to enable them to make way, however slowly. When the multitude of pagodas at Pagan came into view three days and sixty miles later, Phayre was prepared for the formal reception by the King's emissaries, but could hardly have expected the "great retinue of Governors, armed men in thirty boats and two hundred horsemen on the river bank on country ponies, many followed by their foals". Four days were spent exchanging courtesies and seeing the pagodas at Pagan, then for three more days the paddlers plodded on, the river so wide that Yule has remarked on the inability of members of the Mission to identify the mouths of the Chindwin River where it enters the Irrawaddy from the west opposite to Myingyan. This is a puzzle often unsolved by high water season travellers; at least until such time as they have mastered the geography of the countryside, and are able to note landmarks which indicate that the several mouths of the Chindwin flow into the Irrawaddy across a stretch of over twenty miles within that completely flat area.

On 27th August, the Mission reached the appointed rendezvous at Kyauktalon and there awaited the final escort from Amarapoora. When it arrived the sight must have been breathtaking, as no fewer than 150 boats with some 9000 men in royal regalia appeared rowing at great speed down the river. Such a colourful and welcome sight could not have failed to give Phayre yet another indication of the reception he was about to receive and he was further cheered by the arrival on board of Thomas Spears as they steamed into the River Myitnge. By using the "Little River" they were able to moor at a ghaut close to the Residency which had been prepared for the party at Amarapoora.

During their stay of seven weeks at the capital the Mission was lavishly entertained. In the evenings different forms of the Burmese pwé were presented and these sometimes called for considerable endurance on the part of the audience as well as of the players, for they would last many hours into the night. The pwé is the traditional Burmese theatre and takes several different forms, from drama to burlesque, and is invariably accompanied by music which to the unaccustomed ear seems dissonant; and by the very proximity of the honoured guests to the orchestra there is little danger of their being overtaken by drowsiness.

Friendly relations between the King and Phayre were immediately established, but in the end Mindon would not sign any kind of Treaty in case this would imply acceptance by him of the loss for all time of his Pegu Province. While always hoping, and this he continued to do throughout his reign, that if not Arakan and Tenasserim then at least Pegu would be restored to him by the British, he never attempted to recover his lost territory by force; and he did not succeed by persuasion. Lord Dalhousie wrote later that it was his firm conviction that "as a result of the Mission . . . peace with Burma is to the full as secure as any written Treaty could have made it". High praise for the King, for Phayre and not least for Spears.

A portrait of Thomas Spears, drawn by Colesworthy Grant during the stay of the Mission at Amarapoora, carries a description of him as

"the only British resident at Amarapoora, to whom members of the Mission were indebted for many valuable and friendly attentions . . . he was much respected by the King and not less so by his countrymen having at all times honourably maintained his character as an Englishman."

An Englishman from Kirkcaldy! Spears had a Burmese wife and six children, all but the last of whom were born in Amarapoora; the youngest was born in 1859 in Mandalay, where Mindon had built his new capital in 1857.

Thomas Spears remained in his extraordinary two-sided appointment at the capital, retaining always the complete confidence of the King, until 1862, when he settled his family in Rangoon and went to Europe on business. He stayed there until 1867 before returning to Burma, only to die in Rangoon shortly after his return.

So Phayre's Mission to Amarapoora in 1855, while achieving nothing on paper, had achieved much in fact and the Pegu Commissioner returned to Rangoon to his normal duties with a sense of great satisfaction that at long last relations with a Burmese King had been established which had a firm foundation. But this was to last only so long as Mindon was alive; even before the King's death an incredible situation arose to close his doors to British visitors.

The logs of the *Lord William Bentinck* and the *Nerbudda*, recording the eighteen day passage down river from Amarapoora to Rangoon in October 1855, could have applied to a pleasure trip, so absent were any incidents of note. The courtesies of an escort of Burmese war boats was accorded and there was much ceremony at the frontier, but the Mission were clearly in their happiest mood when they tied up at Thayetmyo, where an all-British regiment was included in a garrison composed mainly of East India Company troops from Bengal and Madras.

No account of this fateful period in the story of British rule in Burma would be complete without more about the Governor-General of India at the time. The tenth Earl of Dalhousie was born James Andrew Broun Ramsay in 1812 and succeeded to the earldom in 1838. He was then Member of Parliament for Haddington and continued his political career in the Lords becoming President of the Board of Trade in 1845 in Sir Robert Peel's Government. When he was appointed Governor-General of India in 1848 he was in his thirty-sixth year and the youngest man ever to have held the office. He spent eight years in India, introducing many reforms, implementing momentous decisions, including the annexations of the Punjab and of Oudh, and advancing the building of railways and the policy that they should be, in his own words, "directly but not vexatiously controlled by the government". His role in the annexation of Pegu began with vain attempts to maintain peace with the King of Burma, but when this failed he threw himself into the detail of the campaign in 1852 and "astonished India by the singular genius he exhibited for military organisation" according to the official historian. We have already seen the part he played in two visits to Rangoon in 1852 and how his awareness of the importance of efficient transport led him to order the Irrawaddy Flotilla to be formed. Without it there is little doubt that the annexation of Pegu would have presented serious problems of logistics with a river lifeline of 300 miles.

By remaining in India at the request of the Court of Directors of the East India Company for three years beyond the normal five year term of Governor-General, Dalhousie undermined his already poor health and died four years after returning to his home, Dalhousie Castle in Scotland. He was only forty-eight. In the India Office record of National Biography he was described in 1896 as "one of the greatest, if not the greatest ruler whom India had known."

To Dalhousie's successor, Lord Canning, fell the task of dealing with the India Mutiny, which broke out in 1857, a preoccupation which gave him no time to think about Burma. Internal security in the three Divisions of Arakan, Tenasserim and Pegu was carried on entirely without British troops during the two years it took to suppress the Mutiny, the garrisons of

Indian regiments maintaining peace and loyally serving their British officers. It was not therefore until 1862 that the decision was made to form the three Divisions into the Province of British Burma and hardly surprising that it should remain part of the Indian Empire with a Chief Commissioner responsible to the Viceroy. The East India Company's charter had been revoked after the Mutiny and the Governor-General became the Viceroy.

Arthur Phayre, now a Lieutenant-Colonel, was appointed the first Chief Commissioner of British Burma and immediately set about improving trading relations between the new Province and King Mindon's Burma. He led another Mission to the Court, now at the new capital of Mandalay, in that same year 1862 and secured a commercial Treaty for free trade between the two countries.

The decision to continue Burma's adherence to India on the creation of British Burma is significant to all that follows in this story. Burma was rich in natural resources from which the rulers in India sought to improve their revenues. Had the British Government in London not bowed to the pressures from Calcutta and had set Burma up as a separate British possession, a perfectly logical proposition when one considers the cultural and religious gulfs between the peoples of India and Burma, the history of the eighty years which followed would have been written differently. Yet despite the subjection to India, the trading nation into which the British transformed Burma was prosperous enough and at least it can be said that her security, both international and internal, benefited from the link with India. Against that can be set the one million Indian nationals who settled and made their living in Burma. India undoubtedly made an immense net gain.

CHAPTER FIVE

BHAMO AND THE TRAIL TO CHINA

1. Simon Hannay

Marco Polo, writing of his travels in search of new trade routes, made reference to a trail between the riverine town of Bhamo and the town of Tengyueh (also known as Momein) in the Chinese Province of Yunnan. So far as we know he never saw the trail and it is doubtful if he ever set foot in Burma, but he recorded that Kublai Khan had sent an invading force by this route into the Bhamo District to avenge the murder of the great warrior's envoys at the hands of the King of Burma. This took place in the thirteenth century and from the subsequent absence of any historical mention some six hundred years were to pass before Bhamo was to receive any further notice from the outside world. The Irrawaddy valley in these northern parts, in fact the whole area north of Ava, belonged to the back of beyond.

Major Henry Burney, while British Resident at the Ava Court from 1830 to 1837, formed a burning desire to discover more about the Bhamo / Tengyueh trail and the trade by mule caravans which had used this route for centuries, but he was left in no doubt that King Bagyidaw would not permit any foreigner to proceed up river from Ava, far less into his territory in the far north. Bhamo was thus a closed book officially, but Burney was determined to find some pretext to enable him to send an observer into this unknown land. Several years of his residence were to pass before an opportunity occurred.

From the early eighteenth century hill peoples from the Hukawng Valley and the Burma Hill Tracts, who included Kachins living within the frontiers of Burma, had overspilled into Assam. After the Treaty of Yandabo in 1826, which ceded Assam to British India, these hill migrants became particularly troublesome to the new administration, with consequent embarrassment to the Burmese King who had by the Treaty guaranteed the Assam frontiers with Burma. In 1835 the King came under strong pressure from Assam to subdue groups of Kachins who were making trouble on the border and within

Assam. It was an insurrection, the King knew it and he was embarrassed; and Burney was well aware of his discomfort.

It so happened that a new Myowun was about to depart from Ava to take over the District of Mogaung, north of Bhamo, and the British Resident seized this and the Kachin trouble as the opportunity he was seeking. He proposed to the King that a British officer of his staff, who had special knowledge of the Assam border area, should accompany the Myowun as far as Mogaung and then proceed to the Assam frontier to help in clearing up the ugly situation there. Only as a matter of expedience and to show his concern over the Kachin problem did King Bagyidaw agree.

Thus was Captain Simon Hannay given this assignment and became the first British observer to travel the upper waters of the Irrawaddy. Born in Inverness in 1801, Simon Fraser Hannay was appointed to a cadetship in the Bengal Infantry in 1820 and later as a subaltern he spent much of his service in Assam and on the Assam/Burma border areas. He acquired a keen interest in and considerable knowledge of the Kachin tribes and spoke their language fluently. That he should have been a member of the British Resident's suite at the Court of Ava is perhaps more than a coincidence, but in any event his experience gave Major Burney a strong case for persuading the King to allow him to travel through the jealously guarded northern territory.

At the end of November, 1835, after the flood waters of the high water season had subsided, the Mogaung Governor's party set off from Ava, accompanied by Captain Hannay. The convoy consisted of thirty-four country boats and although they were equipped and ready to use the various means of propulsion common to craft on the river below Ava, the most favoured method in these northern parts was by tracking or rope-towing from the bank of the river.

The diary of the journey left by Hannay reveals his exhilaration at this new experience, quite different from travelling on the lower river. Few and far between were the villages and hamlets as the convoy traversed the long silent reaches, and only one large centre of population at Katha was to be seen on the whole journey of 300 miles to Bhamo. Soon after leaving Ava, the scene changes as the hills close in gradually on the approach to the long forty mile stretch of river known as the Third Defile. There the steep banks deprived the rope-towers of their footholds and the whole convoy took to the oars.

This remarkable stretch of river presents a scene more characteristic of a mountain-girt lake than of a great waterway. It appears to be so shut in at each bend in its course that one wonders if an exit exists at all. The deep water is smooth and placid with the reflections of towering trees from the precipitous banks appearing on the water in dark and ominous shades. Sometimes monkeys in their little family groups escort the boats until such time as they tire of the novelty and disappear into the jungle; sometimes a mahseer rolls over breaking the surface ahead as the rowers disturb the smooth water; but nothing can change the scene of utter peace and serenity. And the final enchantment comes in the cool of the evening when just before sunset the powerful scent of the forest fills the air.

For one hundred miles above the Third Defile the Irrawaddy spreads its course through a wide alluvial plain nurtured by the river in the high water season, but in December flowing slowly between the sandbanks formed in their variety of shapes and sizes as the water recedes. Katha lies to the north of this plain, nestling below the foothills of the mountains which separate the Irrawaddy and Chindwin valleys. It is a straggling town, but presents an imposing appearance from the river, two large pagodas, pure white with gilded domes and spired, standing sentinel amidst the bamboo houses of the mainly Burmese population.

Katha is a market town and Hannay observed the presence of many hill tribes mingling with the Burmese and Chinese shopkeepers and with the townsfolk. He was greatly impressed by the hospitality accorded to the Governor's party, including himself, and by the various pwès presented for their entertainment during their short sojourn of a few days. No doubt his greatest surprise is to be found in the brief comment in his diary that he saw "a tolerable display of British goods for sale in the market". Despite the remoteness of these parts, enterprise was never lacking and it will be seen later that the natives of the far north displayed this quality with great vigour in the river trade.

Fifty miles above Katha and some thirty below Bhamo lies the Second Defile. It is only seven miles in length but presents a majestic scene of rugged beauty, where the great river virtually goes through a mountain. The funnelled waters, narrowed to no more than 300 yards, pass through a winding course taking an almost right-angled bend and are banked at one point by a sheer cliff 800 feet high which plunges straight into the water. It creates a fearsome sight of fast flowing water in the flood season, quite impassable for any type of country boat. For the Governor's convoy it was a hard pull for the rowers, even during this period when the river was at its lowest level, but they were safely through and reached Bhamo as the year drew to a close, one month after they had left Ava.

Major Burney's hopes of information about the little known route into China were only partly satisfied by Hannay's brief visit to Bhamo. The Mogaung Governor was anxious to press on to his destination and allowed a stop of only three days; and this was little enough time for his British passenger to obtain much information about the trail. Burmese merchants in Bhamo treated Hannay with suspicion and it was only through domiciled Chinese, always alert to a trading opportunity, that he gathered sufficient material for a short report to the Resident at Ava. But it was a positive and encouraging report of the volume of traffic already using the route with the traditional mule caravans, ending with "there is a great future for Bhamo, if somebody would do something about it". As time was to show, this was easier said than done.

It is some eighty miles from Bhamo to the mouth of the Mogaung River and within this stretch of the Irrawaddy the First Defile is encountered. Twenty-five miles in length this defile marks the final narrowing of the river after the long wide reach from the Second Defile; this reach widens to over a mile at Bhamo in the flood season. The First Defile is a raging torrent when the river is high, surging down its narrow valley, and for at least six months of the year no craft of any kind could venture upon its waters. Even in the low water season its channels, sometimes no more than 100 feet wide, are defined by rocks and all the skills of the boatmen were put to the test in taking the Governor's convoy through. Beyond this last defile they were soon to leave the Irrawaddy and proceed up the small and tranquil Mogaung River to their destination.

At Mogaung Captain Hannay parted with his host after their six weeks river journey and carried on westward on foot into the Kachin country and to the Assam frontier. His contribution to the story of the Tengyueh trail was small, but it was the first and confirmed its very existence; before there was no more than speculation.

2. Clement Williams

It was only after the Second Burmese War in 1852 and after King Mindon was firmly established on the throne that any interest revived in the possibilities of trade with China through Bhamo. Alternative routes were being suggested and in the hope of settling the matter once and for all, the Calcutta Government sent over to Burma two experienced officials to examine and report on the subject and on commercial problems in general. There was concern at the lack of trade between British Burma and the King's Burma, and Temple and Bruce, the Calcutta officials, recommended that a new attempt should be made to secure a trade Treaty. They dismissed alternative routes into the promising markets of China and urged that trade should be developed via the Bhamo / Tengyueh trail, using the Irrawaddy, and Rangoon as the ocean port. They recommended the creation of a fleet of river steamers, in private hands, to provide the means of transport from Rangoon to Bhamo.

The Temple/Bruce Report was submitted to and accepted by the Viceroy of India in 1860. It was instrumental in bringing about the second Phayre Mission to the Court of Ava in 1862, which as we have already seen led to the signing of a commercial Treaty for free trade between the two countries. The same Treaty provided for the appointment of an official British Resident at Mandalay — Thomas Spears was about to depart for Europe at this time — and included the King's agreement that a British Mission should be allowed to travel up the Irrawaddy to Bhamo. It is a remarkable fact that King Mindon virtually selected the man who was to become British Resident at the Ava Court, making it clear that the appointment of a certain Dr. Clement Williams would invite his pleasure.

Clement Williams, a native of Somerset, qualified in medicine in England and at the age of twenty-four joined the Indian Establishment and was posted as Assistant Surgeon to Her Majesty's 68th Regiment serving at Thayetmyo in Burma. Three years later, having acquired a keen interest in the Burmese people and in the country, he went to Mandalay to spend a furlough in the cool winter season of 1860/61. He had specialised in eye diseases and became known to the King by operations for cataract which he performed while in Upper Burma. The King sent for him and admiration for his medical skill was soon extended to admiration for his knowledge of the Burmese language and for the obviously strong and forthright character of the young doctor. So in 1862, when Mindon was pressed to agree to the appointment of a British Resident at Mandalay, he appears to have had little difficulty in securing the post for Williams, whose qualities had already been noticed by the Chief Commissioner. The King also made it a condition of his agreement to the Bhamo Mission that it should be led by the new Resident; and, to confirm his goodwill, Mindon provided a royal barge and the necessary boats for Williams and his party to make the river journey.

By the terms of the Treaty free trade between Upper and Lower Burma applied no further north than Mandalay. Only British pressure, skillfully handled firstly by Thomas Spears and then by Clement Williams, persuaded the King that an immense trading opportunity with China existed and that free passage to Bhamo from Mandalay was the vital link. But he saw that as a far off prospect and permitted the British expedition partly because of his trust in Williams and partly because he was well aware that the Panthay rebellion in Yunnan would make a sortie on to the trail to Tengyueh dangerous, if not impossible.

The Panthays, who were originally Mohammedans from Central Asia, had inhabited Western Yunnan for centuries and had long been dominant in the citadel capital of Talifoo. They were said to have been brought to Yunnan from their homeland as mercenaries for a Chinese War Lord, had settled and gradually gained power as their numbers increased. Being of Mongolian race like the Yunnanese, they were soon integrated and ethnologically similar in every respect except that they stoutly retained their Mohammedan faith. By the nineteenth century they were *de facto* rulers in Western Yunnan, a situation which eventually stirred the central Chinese Government to greater assertion of their authority and finally precipitated open rebellion by the Panthays. The rebellion broke out in 1855 and was not completely suppressed until 1873, and during these eighteen years the whole area in Yunnan through which the Bhamo/Tengyueh trail passed was unsafe for travellers. The centuries old caravan trade, while not brought to a complete standstill, was seriously curtailed. Yet it appears that this situation was not realised by the British administration in Lower Burma, and not fully by Williams until he arrived in Bhamo and saw for himself. The British Resident believed that he could make a pioneering journey over that trail. He possessed the courage to undertake such a perilous journey, but there was never even a possibility of him being allowed to put it to the test.

Williams left Mandalay in January, 1863 and with the best of river conditions for tracking and rowing made the passage to Bhamo in some twenty days, delaying from time to time only to observe and record details of the course of the river and other information required for the survey which was the main purpose of his expedition. He was courteously received by the Bhamo Myowun, houses were placed at the disposal of his party and every request met, except one. The King had given no instructions for Williams to be permitted to go beyond Bhamo on to the trail to Tengyueh and he had to content himself with collecting all the information available in Bhamo on the terrain of the caravan route. This was to be useful to a later expedition, an account of which will be given in another chapter, but the main value of his journey was in the survey he made of the upper river which in his own words

"contains correct indications of the course of the river, character of country, position and populations of villages on either bank, the islands, shoals, rocks and other features affecting the navigation and trade of the river."

With the firm conclusion that the river was navigable for light draught steamers to Bhamo, Williams added his strong support for the great potential of this route to China and pled for urgency to be given to its development. In this he had the backing of the British commercial communities in Rangoon and Calcutta, not to mention the Manchester Chamber of Commerce, who saw a huge market for their cotton piece goods industry. All the hazards of the trail seem to have been considered as naught, so great were the rewards to be seen from the trade which could be generated with Western China.

The official reaction was also favourable, stimulated no doubt by the intelligence that the French were examining routes into Yunnan from Indo-China; a French expedition via the Mekong River did in fact penetrate into the heart of Yunnan starting from Phnom Penh in 1866, but they took until 1873 to complete their explorations. The British were to travel the Bhamo/Tengyueh trail in 1868. By that time, as we shall see, King Mindon had completely changed his attitude to trade

56

A Burmese Country Boat

The Shwe Dagon Pagoda, Rangoon

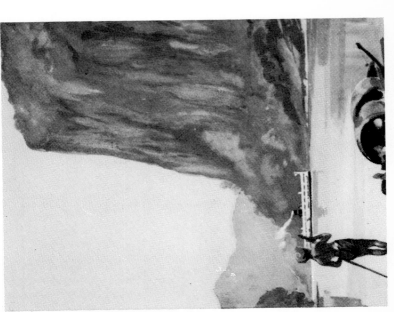

The Second Defile of the Irrawaddy, from an artist's impression

George Swann with Rangoon Office Staff, 1877

Steamer and flat of the Phayre Mission, 1855

above Mandalay and to the possibilities of opening up the route via Bhamo into China.

As for Dr. Clement Williams, he was still in Bhamo in March 1863 gathering information when he was recalled to Mandalay by the King, who wanted the British Resident beside him in dealing with a minor insurrection. Williams was already assuming a major role in the King's Burma, far beyond that of representing the Viceroy and the Chief Commissioner of British Burma at the Court of Ava.

CHAPTER SIX

FLOTILLA COMPANY

Patrick Henderson and Company of Glasgow — in their day "Paddy Henderson" to the seafaring world — had been trading their sailing ships to New Zealand for some ten years when they decided in 1864 that expansion would require more capital than they could command. In these days trade with New Zealand was mainly one way, emigrants and goods from Glasgow out to the new land of opportunity, and the Henderson ships had found profitable return business by running up in ballast from New Zealand to Moulmein and Rangoon to pick up cargoes of rice and teak for Europe. This led to a regular and independent service being started in 1860 between Glasgow and the two Burmese ports.

But the New Zealand trade was growing fast and remained the principal interest; and together with other Scottish business friends Hendersons formed the Albion Shipping Company in 1864 to secure their dominant position as the leading British shipping line in that trade. Interest in New Zealand, however, was not to be all in that eventful year 1864.

The ruling figure in the Henderson partnership then was James Galbraith, a native of Strathaven in Lanarkshire, who had joined the firm as a chartering clerk in 1844 when he was 26 years of age. He had a brilliant brain and used it to such effect that four years later he was made a partner and was soon the moving spirit in the business. The Albion Shipping Company was one result of his enterprise, but at the same time his initiative was being put to an even greater test.

Thomas Findlay of Glasgow, a friend of Galbraith's, was senior partner in the firm of Todd, Findlay and Company, which had been trading since 1839 in the three main ports of the Province of British Burma — Rangoon, Moulmein and Akyab. Their business was the export of rice and teak, but in recent years they had acquired and were operating small steamers on a service down the Tenasserim coast from Moulmein to Victoria

Point, the southern extremity of Burma. James Todd, who ran the Burma business, had fostered this venture and was on the look-out for any opportunity to expand. Not surprising, then, that Todd saw his chance when he learned in 1863 that Colonel Phayre had decided to invite private enterprise to take over the river service between Rangoon and Thayetmyo.

With the approval of the Viceroy of India to the Temple/Bruce Report, the Chief Commissioner also had his own conviction that only thus would trade be able to grow and flourish within the Province and with the King's Burma. He knew from his Irrawaddy journeys that the river was the natural highway of the country and the key to prosperity in both Lower and Upper Burma.

It was late in 1863 when Phayre offered for sale the Irrawaddy Flotilla of four steamers and three flats (one flat presumably having been abandoned in old age to the breaker's yard) together with a five year contract for the carriage of mails, stores and troops between Rangoon and Thayetmyo. After consulting Findlay, Todd made an offer of Rupees 162,000, equivalent then to £16,200, which was accepted and an indenture covering the purchase of the craft and the contract was signed in May, 1864. There were stringent conditions attached to the contract. The Government would pay Rupees 750 per trip for the mails and stipulated rates for stores and troops and they would require sailings twice monthly from Rangoon for Thayetmyo of a steamer and flat within 24 hours of the arrival of the Calcutta mails. The penalty for failure could amount to as much as Rupees 5000.

A number of the Bengal Marine officers of the Flotilla transferred to Todd Findlay's service with their ships and the Chittagonian lascar crews; Todd must have had great confidence in them all to have accepted these conditions with the little fleet of elderly, well worn craft. Wisely he had taken the precaution of securing access to the facilities of the Dalla Dockyard, which was maintained by the Government with slipways and repair equipment adequate for the small, light hulls of the steamers and flats. In this establishment across the river from Rangoon the traditional skills of Burmese shipwrights were employed and the adaptable Burman trained to handle engine repairs.

But it was in weeks rather than months that Todd found that he had bitten off more than he could chew and was warning

Findlay that any prospect of success would require more capital — much more — and a concentration of effort on the operation of the Flotilla, neither of which he was able to provide. Findlay turned to his friend James Galbraith, and with Peter Denny, the Dumbarton shipbuilder and a leading shareholder in the Albion Shipping Company, the three formed a syndicate to take over the Irrawaddy Flotilla and the contract with the ultimate objective of floating a public Company. This objective was rapidly achieved and in December, 1864, a Notice to Shareholders was issued by the new Company, the Irrawaddy Flotilla and Burmese Steam Navigation Company Limited, which informed them that the steamers and flats, and the contract, would be taken over by the Company on 1st January, 1865. *(See Appendix)*

Galbraith's strategy is clear. The new Company would provide a link with the Henderson ships already trading between the United Kingdom and Burma, not only up the Irrawaddy with the Flotilla but also across the Gulf of Martaban to Moulmein with the towing steamer *Ava,* which had also been acquired from Todd Findlay. The Notice, obviously the product of Galbraith's pen, strikes an optimistic note of the prospects for the new Company and it seems that Todd was making profits. But he saw that this would not last without capital to acquire new ships and without more human resources, which he could not afford.

It could hardly be said that James Galbraith indulged in short cuts when he was party to a name like "The Irrawaddy Flotilla and Burmese Steam Navigation Company, Limited" — it became known as the Flotilla Company or just the I.F. — but his impatience with the problems of the early years of the new Company is only too evident in his letters to the Agents in Burma, in which capacity Todd, Findlay and Company remained. A setback occurred before the Flotilla Company was even in business. James Todd had gone to Calcutta late in 1864 to purchase light draught vessels to augment the tottering Irrawaddy Flotilla, but was lost at sea while returning to Rangoon in a disaster which overtook the British India Company's ship *Persia.* He was the key man in Burma and a heavy responsibility, and much of James Galbraith's wrath, fell upon his successor, John McColl. For example:—

"I need hardly tell you that the results hitherto have been

very discouraging — and starting with a very loud trumpet blast we are now humiliatingly performing on a penny whistle! ... we have a bare dividend of five per cent for 1865 ... it is very problematical whether the trade of the river will be sufficiently expansive for a considerable length of time to make the returns of the Company as remunerative as they ought to be ... Denny and my firm have had to advance a considerable sum which is not convenient for us in our large business to be long out of ... Ways and Means never seem to bother you East India Nabobs!"

Thus a letter from Galbraith to McColl in 1866 and the following year a lengthy correspondence between them argued the best way to maintain the service to Moulmein in the face of competition from the powerful British India Company. There were more lusty broadsides from Galbraith, including a reminder to McColl that "better a finger aff as aye waggin'" before they decided to "stick to the river". Only the complete lack of hope of profitable trading persuaded Galbraith and his colleagues in Glasgow to surrender the service between Rangoon and Moulmein to the B.I.

McColl was a worthy successor to Todd and laid some firm foundations before that first year 1865 was very old. He took delivery of two steamers acquired in Calcutta by Todd and maintained the Government contract without default; he used to the full his position as General Manager of Todd, Findlay and Company to advance the interests of the new venture; and, perhaps most significantly, he appointed Dr. Clement Williams as Agent of the Flotilla Company at Mandalay. The two had met in 1864 when McColl visited Mandalay and the British Resident had given McColl an account of the navigation and commercial possibilities of the river between Mandalay and Bhamo. When Williams was recalled to his regiment in 1865 on completing his term as Resident at Mandalay, he resigned his commission rather than return to the routine of army-life, went to see McColl and was soon back in Mandalay as the first Agent of the new Company.

The Government contract had run less than three years when James Galbraith asked McColl to approach the Chief Commissioner for some increase in the rates. Colonel Phayre was sympathetic, having seen a new steamer (which incidentally bore his name) and ten new flats added to the fleet during 1865 and 1866. The *Colonel Phayre,* constructed at A. & J. Inglis' shipyard in Glasgow and re-erected at Dalla Dockyard, was the first paddler built for the I.F. and began the replacement of the "old rubbish" — Galbraith's description of the original Irrawaddy Flotilla. The flats were built at Dalla.

Phayre received from McColl a memorandum shortly before his retiral in March, 1867 and this was followed up by a meeting between him and Galbraith in London. Later, writing to Galbraith, Sir Arthur Phayre — he had received the distinction of Knight Commander of the Star of India on retiral — gave some good advice:—

"As I am no longer Chief Commissioner of British Burma I cannot undertake to say what view my successor might take of this question, but I think I may presume that what I have stated will be acknowledged to be consistent with the interests of Government and of the public. My view is that a Steam Navigation Company should exist on the Irrawaddy and that if it can be made clear to Government that the existing contract has not been reasonably profitable to the Company then I feel confident that Government would alter the contract ..."

The new Chief Commissioner was Colonel Albert Fytche, another product of the Bengal Army and Commissioner of the Tenasserim Division in Burma since 1857. He agreed with Phayre and proceeded to review the Company's contract, with satisfactory result. Even more importantly, he went to Mandalay and found King Mindon ready to conclude a much more liberal trade treaty than ever before, including freedom for British steamers to conduct a regular service between Rangoon and Mandalay and also between Mandalay and Bhamo. It was therefore as another tribute to the Chief Commissioner's office that when a second new paddler was completed in late 1867 she was named *Colonel Fytche.*

The Flotilla was now sufficiently strong in numbers to deploy one of the new paddlers to run through to Mandalay from Rangoon on a regular service and with yet another steamer commissioned in 1868 a fortnightly service began. This latest addition to the fleet, the *Mandalay,* was 245 feet in length, had compound engines and was the first paddler capable of towing two flats, one at each sponson (paddle box). Built on the Clyde by Duncans to a new design by Dennys and re-erected at Dalla, she brought a new dimension in power and speed to the Irrawaddy. But, tragedy of tragedies, she was only a few months old when she went aground on a falling river, broke her back and was a total wreck. This loss delayed the start of the service from Mandalay to Bhamo until 1869 when the *Colonel Fytche* was stationed at Mandalay and opened a monthly service on the upper river.

Dr. Clement Williams was now well established as the Flotilla Company's man at Mandalay. His friendship with King Mindon and his experience and understanding of the Burmese enabled him to exert a special influence for the Company at the Court and to play an important part in the development of the whole operation. He had been highly critical of the design of the two *Colonel* paddlers, advocating that a ship suitable for the Irrawaddy should have

"no external keel, bows after the model of the narrow end of a soup spoon and sixty feet added to length . . . no use a winch intended to do a capstan's work — in the upper Irrawaddy especially it is impossible always to avoid grounding and a good strong means of applying dragging power is most necessary."

They were words of hard experience which did not go unheeded when the *Mandalay* was designed, and her successors were to follow the new pattern. But there were no immediate successors, as there was a marking of time for four years until 1872 and while trade was on the increase and every steamer and flat fully employed, the policy was to consolidate and commit no further capital for the time being.

In the meantime, having put the first of the new capital to work, Galbraith was looking out for a suitable man to send out to Burma to manage the growing operation. He wrote to McColl in October, 1867:—

"At last I have got you a good man for the practical working of the steamers — Mr. James Wilson. He has been trained in two of our steam Companies here and I feel sure he will put matters in a better working shape. Subject to your supervision, he must be master of the position — I have told him that he will have entire charge under you. He sails today in our *Helen Burns* — we could not get a berth in the P. & O. until December and by the H.B. he will be out sooner and a good deal of money saved."

A berth in the P. & O. was, however, occupied by

"a young gentleman from our office, who has been assistant bookkeeper for some years and having the I.F. Coy's accounts through his hands he knows the way in which I would like your Books for the Company kept — I think it of consequence to have a Clerk in your establishment separate for the use of Mr. Wilson."

The young gentleman was George Jameson Swann, the son of a Supervisor of Inland Revenue, born and brought up in Perthshire. By the time George went to work in Patrick Henderson's office the Swann family had moved to Glasgow and he left his home there at the age of 27 to go out to Burma with a good sound education in him, an equally sound training in shipping and the keeping of accounts according to the requirements of James Galbraith, and above all the reliable background of a good Scottish middle class family. He was, and remained, a bachelor all his life.

The Burma climate did not suit James Wilson and when his health began to fail George Swann made sure that he was ready to step in and take charge of the Flotilla. He soon became designated as an Assistant and by 1870 was virtually in command, with two more British Assistants sent out to join him. Ill health forced James Wilson to resign and leave Burma for good in 1871, so at the age of 31 George Swann became Manager of Flotilla Company operation within the agency of Todd, Findlay and Company. He had prepared and presented to the Board of Directors in Glasgow a three year plan for expansion of the fleet, with seven new paddlers of the *Mandalay* class and eighteen more flats — the technique of keeping the steamers moving and leaving the flats at various stations on the river to load or discharge had been developed, requiring a considerable availability of the relatively inexpensive flats, which were in the main built at Dalla Dockyard.

Swann's plan was accepted and in 1872 fresh capital was sought. The prospectus issued to existing shareholders gave an optimistic report of the river trade and of the outlook for the future; the new capital was immediately subscribed and by 1875 the fleet consisted of eleven steamers and thirty-two flats, with all the "old rubbish" discarded. Two new British Assistants had been trained in Glasgow and sent out to Burma, British certificated deck and engineer officers engaged and more lascar seamen recruited and brought over from Chittagong. A long term lease of Dalla Dockyard had been secured and the course for the future was truly set.

But it could hardly be expected that all was plain sailing, even metaphorically speaking. One of the problems, of which no doubt there were many, was described in a letter written in February, 1872, to James Galbraith by David Mair, successor to John McColl as Manager of Todd Findlay. After expressing concern at news received from Galbraith that competition for the steamer trade, which already existed in a small way from three sternwheelers built in Italy for King Mindon, was about to be intensified with the arrival of six more of the same type, Mair was writing:—

"According to report they are coming out on account of the King. An Engineer is also on the way out to superintend the fitting together of them, which is to be done at Mandalay, and in this is the chief gleam of hope. It is quite likely that this Engineer will be ordered to put the boats together without money or men provided and that unable to surmount the difficulties will retire in disgust. However, if the boats are put together and remain in the possession of the Ministers the opposition will not be so powerful as were they in hands of European Agents, which would be a matter of grave anxiety."

The six sternwheelers were eventually re-erected at Mandalay, but the King's fleet of nine seems to have had no noticeable effect on the river trade and the conclusion must be reached that they suffered from the start from lack of care and maintenance. The King did use them for trading when they were in service but he sometimes used them for his entertainment; he used to race them! An unlikely story exists that the first three sternwheelers were sent out from Italy with the materials for the new Mandalay Palace when it was being decorated by Venetian craftsmen. Mindon moved his capital to Mandalay in 1857, long before the Suez Canal was opened, and the passage of light-draughted stern-wheelers round the Cape of Good Hope would be, to say the least, extremely hazardous.

The opening of the Suez Canal in 1869 had led Patrick Henderson and Company to the decision to start a steamer service between Glasgow, Liverpool and Rangoon and by 1872 this had brought increased trade with Burma. It all fitted in with Swann's plan and as the new units arrived during the years 1872 to 1874 the traffic was virtually waiting for them to be commissioned. The real expansion was about to begin and preparations were going ahead to mount a much larger operation. At the Annual Meeting of the Company in Glasgow in May, 1875, the Chairman intimated that

"the business of the Company having greatly outgrown the anticipations of the original promoters, the powers conferred by the Articles of Association were found to be too limited for the proper working of the Company under the existing circumstances, the Directors recommend that a new Company should be formed under a broader basis under amended Articles of Association."

On 1st January 1876, with the name changed to simply *Irrawaddy Flotilla Company Limited,* the business took on a new look. The next ten years were to see great changes; George Swann became the first Manager of the new Company; Dennys of Dumbarton, having examined the problems of Irrawaddy navigation through visits to Burma by William Denny and John McAusland, both Directors of the shipbuilding company and of the Flotilla Company, began to build the steamers, ousting Duncan. And the Henderson house flag, the French tricolour reversed with the Union Jack in the centre of the white band, replaced the original, a peacock in his pride encircled in a green background. The link-up was complete; the Henderson ships carried out to Burma not only the growing British trade but also the river steamers from the Denny yard for re-erection at Dalla and steel for the building of flats; they carried the men who were joining the Flotilla and those travelling on leave; and in a very short time Todd Findlay found it expedient to resign the Agency in Rangoon and thus give Swann the freedom he sought to set up a full and independent establishment, devoted entirely to the management of the Company.

CHAPTER SEVEN

ACROSS THE TRAIL

We now have to return to the trail into China from Bhamo which had excited so much interest in both Government and commercial circles in British Burma and India. The outcome of all the effort, not to mention the intrigue and lobbying, which was expended on this short but vital link in the route to Western Yunnan via the Irrawaddy, promised to be highly advantageous for the river trade. The scene, therefore, would not be complete without some description of the trail and of its origin.

First it has to be clear that there is no connection between the trail from Bhamo and either of the two roads which have traversed parts of Upper Burma in recent times. The famous Burma Road was built in the late 1930's from the Burma Railways railhead at Lashio in the Southern Shan States to Kunming in Western China. It was one answer to Japan's invasion of the Chinese mainland and the closure of the ports on her eastern seaboard, and carried a heavy traffic until the Japanese overran Burma in 1942. The Ledo Road was built by the American General Stilwell from Ledo in Assam to Myitkyina on the Irrawaddy, 100 miles north of Bhamo, in the latter part of the war with Japan of 1941-45 when the Allies had re-taken that northern area of Burma.

There is no doubt that caravans were on the trail from Bhamo to Tengyueh long before it attracted the attention of Marco Polo in the thirteenth century. And it seems certain that the *modus operandi,* quite primitive, has remained unchanged over the centuries. The track itself can only be described as a rough bridle path fashioned by the tramp of countless feet — human, mules and horses — and in places by the effect of constant erosion by water. It follows roughly the line of the Taping River, which joins the Irrawaddy two miles north of Bhamo and then of the Takaw River, a tributary of the Taping, with spurs and gradients making the going extremely hard. Neither river can be used even by the smallest craft, so rocky and tumbling are their courses. Sometimes the trail surmounts hills, often to reach small hill-top settlements of Kachins, or sometimes Shans, havens for tired caravans. Only four villages of any size are to be found on the whole of the 135 miles from Bhamo to Tengyueh. Tengyueh itself is a walled city, well situated as a centre for communication to the east and the vastness of China and less than 100 miles from Talifoo, the provincial capital of Western Yunnan. The nineteenth century had brought roads connecting the two citadel towns and the neighbouring territory to the eastwards, again emphasising the absolute nature of the break in the link between the Irrawaddy and China, which only an effective opening of the route from Bhamo to Tengyueh would resolve.

Traffic on the trail can be conducted only by pack mules, which carry the merchandise, and always move in caravans for safety; there are occasional ponies for the rare traveller who can afford such luxury. Such is the terrain that it is impossible to use any vehicle on wheels. The mules are controlled by a tough breed of Chinese muleteers, rugged men who drive their animals to the point of exhaustion; the leanness of the mules and the extent of the back sores which attract continuous swarms of the ubiquitous fly, reflect the struggle for survival.

Then there is the ever present danger from the bands of dacoits who not only roam these parts but frequently establish themselves, by sheer brutality, in control of tracts of country. It is a situation which could instill fear into the most intrepid and must conjure up in the mind visions of the hardships endured and dangers faced by these courageous British pioneers of the nineteenth century.

Cotton and salt, plentiful in Burma, were much in demand in Yunnan and were the main commodities carried from Bhamo to Tengyueh; and as manufactured cotton goods found their way up the river to Bhamo in increasing quantities this became a large part of the trade. From the Chinese side raw silk was practically the only traffic; generally the caravans travelled westwards almost light. And with or without the connivance of such border control as existed, there was a continuous, and of course illegal, movement of opium across the whole operation.

Clement Williams was replaced as British Resident at the

Court of Ava in 1865 by Captain Edward Sladen, an officer of the Madras Fusiliers who had first seen service in Burma during the war of 1852. The new Resident came from an East India Company family, his father being a doctor in the Madras Establishment when Edward was born there in 1827. After schooling in England he followed the family tradition and returned to a military cadetship in India.

Sladen had stayed on in Burma after the conclusion of the 1852 war, having been selected as an Assistant Commissioner and posted to the Administration in Tenasserim. He was back with his regiment for service in the Indian Mutiny in 1857/8, but reverted to District work in Burma in 1860. His appointment to Mandalay in 1865 was ample proof of the qualities he possessed and he seemed then to be destined for the highest office; yet the progress of his career thereafter was slow. As events to follow will show, he was something of a hard-liner on British policy in Upper Burma and this appears to have been evident during the five years of his Residency at the Ava Court.

His personal relationship with King Mindon was always openly cordial, but when he was gone his successor recorded this comment on him, made by the King during an audience:—

"I am not against him. Good people are liked and have good repute; bad people are disliked and people will speak ill of them. No one, not even I, can gag public opinion. I never heard anyone speak ill of Phayre, which proves he is good and estimable ... Rotten fruit will stink, no matter how much perfume you may pour on it! In speaking as I do now of Sladen I simply reflect public opinion."

Some of the subtlety of this royal utterance may be lost in the translation, but the meaning is clear. Yet there is also evidence that Mindon held him in high regard. Edward Sladen may not have always observed the diplomatic niceties to the letter, but he was then already accumulating a knowledge and understanding of Burma, her people and the language which were to be vitally important to British policy-making twenty years later.

The Resident had an early opportunity to show his resourcefulness in 1866 when King Mindon faced an insurrection. Three of the royal princes were murdered, including his chosen heir, and the situation was tense. There were menacing disturbances and Sladen gathered together all the

Europeans in Mandalay, commandeered a Flotilla Company steamer and brought them all safely down river to British territory.

But it is with his courageous sortie into Yunnan that we are now concerned. Sladen was present with Chief Commissioner Fytche when the commercial Treaty of 1867 was concluded with King Mindon at Mandalay and was the pressure man for the establishment of the steamer service to Bhamo. Not only was this successfully negotiated, but so also was the right to instal a British Political Agent at Bhamo and freedom to explore the trail into Yunnan.

With the ink on the Treaty barely dry Sladen made his plans to go to Bhamo himself and to take with him Clement Williams, by then I. F. Company Agent at Mandalay; Dr. Anderson, a naturalist from the British Administration in Rangoon; and a small escort drawn from the garrison of Indian troops at the Mandalay Residency. The King was now actively encouraging the expedition and placed the *Yenan Sekia,* one of his Italian built sternwheelers, at the disposal of the party. In Sladen's own words:—

"The expedition which I had the honour to command left Mandalay by steamer on 13th January, 1868. One of our objects in proceeding by steamer was to test the navigability of the Irrawaddy for steam traffic beyond or above the capital. Hitherto no steamer had ever ascended the river as far north as Bhamo, and the Burmese Government had publicly declared that no steamer could possibly do so at that time, or during certain seasons of the year, when the river was said to be at its lowest depth. Our steamer, however, the draft of which did not exceed three feet, reached Bhamo without difficulty of any kind in river navigation; and the result of our trip proved generally that the Irrawaddy is navigable for steamers of moderate draft at all seasons of the year, as far north as Bhamo, a distance of 900 miles from our starting point at the port of Rangoon, and 300 miles above the Royal capital town of Mandalay."

The river journey took eight days and the King's steamer seems to have been navigated well enough, yet Sladen's only adverse comment was reserved for the crew who were described as "raw Burmans, quite slovenly and disinterested" — possibly truthful, but hardly the words of a diplomat, especially when they got there — and back. From Dr. Anderson came the report of a delighted naturalist, who had time during a leisurely journey to collect orchids and other rare plants and to make copious notes on the fauna and the tropical forests of this fascinating stretch of river. On the Second Defile his comment was emphatic — "the scenery of this defile or gorge surpasses anything I have ever beheld."

There was a delay for Sladen of five weeks at Bhamo awaiting the local Myowun's approval to proceed on the trail to Tengyueh. Fears that the party might be ambushed by Kachins before crossing into China were allayed only after sending out officials to parley with the Kachin headmen along the route and bargain with freedom for the Kachins to enter Bhamo, from where they had been forbidden. The Sladen party would not have gone far on that trail without the King's sanction and the efforts of the Bhamo Myowun.

On 26th February, accompanied by a mule caravan carrying their supplies, they set off on the 135 miles journey, fraught with many dangers on both the Burma side and in Yunnan, where the Panthays were still in rebellious control. The Kachins, regarded as primitive by the more civilised Burmese, occupied much of the attention of the party in the early part of their trek. Sladen wrote of them:—

"Under proper treatment, they proved to be kind and intelligent, with a certain admixture of truth and treachery ... they are keen traders, work cheerfully for gain and are hospitable to strangers. Their religion consists solely in the propitiation of good and evil spirits, by sacrifices and observances too numerous to mention. Curiosity is legend. There was absolutely no relief, in eating, drinking, reading, writing, washing, dressing and undressing. It was in vain to attempt privacy. The glaring curiosity of these unsatisfied gazers was a positive affliction, forgotten happily for a time, though by no means terminated, even in sleep."

Sladen himself was involved in rituals, on one occasion by a death dance, on another by a trance, and he could never understand the indiscriminate firing of guns that often took place, even inside houses he was occupying, for no apparent

71

reason whatever.

Sladen tells of his party's arrival at Ponsee, the last village in Burma on the route "which is ever memorable to us as the scene of our weary detention of more than two months". Every obstacle was put in their way — "the roads are held by armed men" and "brigand chief Lee Sheetahee holds the Pass at Mauphoo" — but they were not frightened off and eventually wore down all attempts to stop their progress.

When they crossed into Yunnan, disorders arising from the Panthay rebellion kept their escort constantly on the alert, but as they came nearer to their destination offers of assistance from settlements along the route were evidence that news had gone ahead of the progress of their caravan. The Panthay Governor of Tengyueh had sent orders down the trail for their safety and succour and as they approached the walls of the town they received a remarkable welcome, with troops lining their path in full State dress.

It was the end of May, 1868, when the British party, the first white men to have crossed the trail from Bhamo, marched into Tengyueh. They stayed seven weeks, making agreements for the safe conduct of caravans once the rebellion had finally succeeded, which the Panthays confidently expected. But they proved to be wrong and one must wonder at the wisdom of making agreements with a rebel Government, with the obvious repercussions which might arise with the Chinese Central Government. No doubt the answer lay in the fact that by that time the Panthays had been in control of Western Yunnan for thirteen years and were to stay that way for another five. It looked then like a permanent situation. Sladen also made agreements "to facilitate trade, with every person or chief who had any semblance of authority in the region traversed", which on the bare facts appear to have been even less soundly based.

But we have to remember that this was the first British penetration into the much sought after route into China, made with almost unbelievable risks by these courageous men and they were bringing back every possible assurance that would encourage trade to be developed. Sladen concluded his report with words which would make it hard for anyone to question the success of the expedition:—

"My firm conviction is that, despite all obstacles and all retarding influences of whatever nature, the prospective results of our expedition will reveal themselves in time by a vast increase to the trade of Burmah by free commercial overland intercourse between Burmah and China, and by tardy but cordial recognition of our services by the country at large. It is important to bear in mind the particular configuration of the country which intervenes at this point between Bhamo and the Chinese frontier, for it solves in great measure the very important problem of an overland trade route connecting these two countries and proves moreover that the Burmese and Chinese populations and Governments, at a time when trade flourished in these parts, had both observed, and availed themselves of the natural advantages of position and facilities for transit, which were presented to them by following these valleys, which by directness of course, general inclination and position, so invitingly held out the means of inter-communication and commercial intercourse between their respective countries. It is further interesting too, to note this configuration, because it discloses a geographical certainty which nothing but exploration could possibly have solved."

There is not a word to be found of the return journey either on the trail or down river from Bhamo to Mandalay, where they arrived late in September 1868, after an absence of more than eight months — a very long time for Mandalay to be without the British Resident and the Flotilla Company without their Agent.

In the following year, 1869, the final part of the 1867 Treaty was implemented by the appointment of Captain G. A. Strover as Political Agent at Bhamo. Strover left Mandalay to take up his appointment on the *Colonel Fytche,* the first Flotilla Company steamer to ply the Mandalay / Bhamo waters and then opening a monthly service. As the main purpose of having the Political Agent at Bhamo was to stimulate the trade through to China, Strover took with him a party of Rangoon merchants complete with samples of their wares — a veritable Trade Mission. Within safe distances from Bhamo the Mission was highly successful, but far into the trail was no place for a peace-loving boxwallah and little progress was made then or in the following four years selling British goods to Yunnan.

In 1873, when the Panthay rebellion was finally suppressed and security on the trail much improved, Strover successfully promoted trade to Tengyueh and was instrumental in persuading the Flotilla Company to operate the service from Mandalay fortnightly. Unfortunately, the obviously active Strover had been involved in the supply of arms to the Panthay Governor of Tengyueh, to which the Chinese Central Government not unnaturally took exception, and he received a posting to Lower Burma. That his years in Bhamo were otherwise well spent there can be no doubt and he left a situation full of promise for a great trade with Yunnan.

In London, the British Associated Chambers of Commerce lost no time in petitioning the Secretary of State for India, who was then Lord Salisbury, for a fresh survey to be made of the route from Bhamo to Tengyueh. It was the age of the railway and Sladen had recommended that the possibility should be examined when more peaceful conditions prevailed on the trail. The time was ripe.

The Chinese Government in Pekin were co-operative and Lord Salisbury decided in 1874 that there should be a double expedition to Tengyueh, one party setting out from Shanghai and the other from Mandalay via Bhamo. The Shanghai party, led by Augustus Margary of the British Consulate at Shanghai, made such a spectacular journey from Shanghai right through to Bhamo that they arrived there before the Burma party. The latter had taken a circuitous overland route from Mandalay and had been delayed. Led by Colonel Horace Browne, an experienced Burma administrator, they had not reckoned with the speed achieved by Margary from far off Shanghai.

Finding that Browne had not yet reached Bhamo, Margary set off back along the Tengyueh trail to make preparations for him at the frontier. His eagerness cost him his life. Moving ahead of his military escort, he was murdered by Chinese tribesmen who had learned that the expedition was the forerunner of a railway, which they did not want. By this time Browne had passed through Bhamo and he in turn was ambushed by Chinese and was forced to return to Bhamo. He had rescued the remainder of the Shanghai party and all joined the first steamer from Bhamo for Mandalay.

Further attempts to establish the case for a railway met with no response from the Government of India and without something better than a mule trail the real potential of trade through Burma to China was never exploited to the full. There were serious doubts on the practicability of a railway, but perhaps more important to the British decision to do nothing was the knowledge that the French had failed in their efforts to find a trade route into Yunnan via Indo-China. The steamer service to Bhamo continued and grew as the years went on, but the interest in the China trade by this route seems to have died with Augustus Margary in 1875.

The mule caravans still walk the Bhamo/Tengyueh trail today.

CHAPTER EIGHT

KING THEBAW ... AND FRED KENNEDY

The new Irrawaddy Flotilla Company of 1876 began its life with eleven modern paddle steamers and thirty-two flats, a compact little fleet concentrating the whole effort on the one thousand miles of the main Irrawaddy River from Rangoon to Bhamo. A change of route out of Rangoon, necessitated by the size of the newest type of paddler towing two flats, had added 100 miles to the passage: the direct Panhlaing Creek route was abandoned in favour of the deeper tidal Bassein Creek which joined the Rangoon River to the China Bakir some fifteen miles below Rangoon, close to the open sea.

Government contracts were still being met by the Company within British Burma and keen exchanges took place whenever contracts came up for renewal, but financial returns had become more dependent on revenues from the carriage of ordinary commercial traffic. And it was on this growing trade in cargo and passengers, which the steamers themselves generated, that the future expansion of the fleet was firmly founded. There were, however, many problems and a good deal of trouble to be encountered and endured during the first decade which followed that year 1876.

King Mindon's long reign had seen an encouraging improvement in relations between Upper and Lower Burma, but sad to relate it was an uncharacteristic action by the British — perhaps not so to those who chose to label the Victorians as arrogant! — which severed the valuable link with King Mindon in 1875. The Indian Government decided that the British Resident in Mandalay should no longer remove his shoes when being received by the Burmese King. This was a ritual of respect, quite indispensable in traditional Burmese custom. An instruction was issued, applicable to all British officers, and does not appear to have been called in question by the Chief Commissioner of British Burma of the time. Names are better left out of this pathetic incident; Fytche had retired as Chief

Commissioner and Sladen had long since left Mandalay for another appointment, but what can safely be said is that neither of them, nor Sir Arthur Phayre, would have approved of the discourtesy, if nothing else, shown by this apparently trivial order. The inevitable result was that no British officer, including the Resident, was received by Mindon for the last three years of his life, a high price to pay and all the less justified if the reason given for the decision by at least one historian is correct. It is said that during a visit to Calcutta earlier in 1875 the Prince of Wales, future King Edward VII and King Emperor of India, received envoys from the Burmese King and that they were invited to sit on chairs and to wear shoes. From this it was deduced that British envoys could not therefore be allowed to remove their shoes at the Court of Ava. There must have been another, and one would hope, better reason.

Little wonder that, with this absence of personal contact with the King, incidents began to occur up and down the river where the Flotilla Company steamers plied in Upper Burma. It soon became common knowledge that the British no longer had the ear of the King and could be treated like anyone else. One such incident involved Captain Doyle who was in command of the *Chindwin*, one of the Company's new paddle steamers. He had arrived up in Mandalay on the regular run from Rangoon and having seen to the safe mooring of his steamer and flats he went ashore to report to the Agent at his office near the river. It was the high water season, with the steamer ghauts high on the bund which protected the Mandalay shore area from the river, and the going was muddy and slippery from recent rains. The Captain decided to make a detour to the office to avoid the mud and unwittingly trespassed on sacred ground. He was immediately arrested by Burmese police and clapped into stocks and in this situation he remained for two hours until the Agent was found and tactfully arranged for the Captain's release.

More later of the Agent, an Italian named Andreino, who had been appointed in 1872 when Dr. Clement Williams left the Company's service. As for Williams, after three years as British Resident and seven as the Flotilla Company Agent, the great esteem in which he was held by the King resulted in his being made a Minister of State at the Ava Court. He held this appointment until after the King's death in 1878.

King Mindon died without having named his successor. One heir-apparent had been murdered in the insurrection of 1866, leaving him afraid to nominate another favoured son, and palace intrigue had continued among his immense progeny. Fifty-three wives had given him no less than forty-eight sons and sixty-two daughters and the wives led the plotting for their sons to gain the throne. But it was the Centre Queen who proved to have the greatest skill at this activity. With no sons, she married her daughter Supayalat to the Thebaw Prince, son of a minor Queen, and conspired successfully with the Kinwun Mingyi (Chief Minister) to put Thebaw on the throne. Then to thwart any attempts to supplant him, Thebaw was persuaded to order the massacre of all the other princes who could be seized. Some of the genuine contenders for the throne had already fled to British Burma for safety, but over forty of the royal family were said to have been done to death one fateful night within the grounds of the palace, while their screams for mercy were drowned by continual and loud playing of pwé music all night.

The British Residency in Mandalay played a vital part when the turmoil created by this massacre erupted in Upper Burma and shocked the world. Not that it was the first time that the elimination of possible contenders for the throne had taken place in Burma, but it was the first time that it had happened since the British had occupied Lower Burma and since there had been a telegraph system to flash the news across the globe. The British Resident Shaw protested and conveyed protests from both Rangoon and Calcutta, but the shoe question was still alive and the nearest approach he had to the King was through the Kinwun Mingyi, who merely reminded him of the independence of Thebaw's kingdom. With relations seriously strained, the harbouring in the Residency of some of the royal survivors of the purge who had been smuggled out of the palace did not help the anti-British attitude of the King and his Ministers, among whom only Clement Williams condemned the slaughter. Williams had become the medium of day to day communication between the British Resident and the palace clique and had helped to protect the Residency and British lives, but he was so shocked by the reign of terror under Thebaw that he took his leave of the new King and departed for Rangoon and England.

Clement Williams had been over twenty years in Burma without a break and longed to return to his native Somerset, only loyalty and affection for King Mindon keeping him from taking leave long before. Now he had no heart for remaining a Minister. But his health was undermined and he contracted typhoid and died at Naples in June 1879 while on his way to England.

If it can be termed a monument, the house he built in 1868 at Mandalay shore, a short distance from the river, still stood eighty years later fulfilling the purpose for which Williams intended it, the home of the Flotilla Company Agent. Later to become the Agency Office, a single storey building stood at the entrance to the long drive to the house. With walls of bricks and mortar four feet thick, this edifice was built as an ice factory for King Mindon.

The departure of Clement Williams from Mandalay severed the last link between the Court of Ava and the British Residency and it seems to have been all too much for Resident Shaw who, already afflicted with heart trouble, died at his post in June 1879. He was succeeded by the ill-fated Colonel Horace Browne, whose attempt to reach Tengyueh in 1875 had ended in disaster. Browne was no more successful in Mandalay, finding relations with the King and his Ministers so strained that reconciliation was impossible. After two months he withdrew with most of his staff to Rangoon, leaving a chargé d'affaires, with the Residency in a state almost amounting to seige. When in September news reached Rangoon of the murder in Kabul of the Resident there and his entire staff, it was decided to take no further risk with British lives in Mandalay and the Residency was closed.

Many incidents continued to hamper the running of the river steamers and much provocation had to be met with patient response. Each one had an alarming and demoralising effect on the Captains and other British officers serving on the river and there was to be a long and critical period in this atmosphere of apprehension. It persisted throughout King Thebaw's reign of seven years.

But trade went on, growing mainly in British Burma. The railway from Rangoon to Prome, Burma's first, had been opened in 1877 and the Flotilla Company began operating a daily ferry service between Prome and Thayetmyo to link with the frontier station. By 1880 the Company had a fleet of twenty-two steamers and thirty-eight flats and had started the first regular service in the delta, from Rangoon to Bassein; many were to follow and open up this vast maze of creeks for steam navigation. And despite the absence of diplomatic exchanges with Thebaw's Court and the provocations frequently encountered, the I.F. and other British Companies stoically continued with their business in Upper Burma and made their own contacts and commercial arrangements with the King and his Ministers.

Before we come to the climax of King Thebaw's reign we have to retrace our steps to 1877, the year which saw the arrival in Burma of Frederick Charles Kennedy, the man who was to follow George Swann as Manager of the Irrawaddy Flotilla Company.

Swann's right-hand man and Assistant Manager, Archibald Colquhoun, had died suddenly in Rangoon in October, 1877, at the early age of thirty, and the search for a successor began at once in Scotland. Kennedy was selected, agreed to sail without delay and was in Rangoon before the end of the year. He was engaged by James Galbraith and his first and later service contracts with the Company — he immediately became Assistant Manager over the heads of Assistants already serving in Burma — show that he possessed qualities and experience which had to be recognised and, in more materialistic terms, paid for.

Kennedy was an Edinburgh man, born in 1848 in Leith where his father was a tweed merchant. He had no inclination to join his father in business and when the time came for him to earn his living he decided to become a civil engineer. But having qualified he was dissatisfied with his progress and financial prospects, believing that he would have to look beyond the borders of Scotland if his ambitions were to be fulfilled. The Irrawaddy Flotilla Company was his opportunity and he seized it.

For two men of such strong personality and outstanding ability, it was fortunate that Fred Kennedy immediately established an excellent relationship with Swann, who gave him every opportunity to learn the workings of the Company. First he took over as cashier and soon came to understand how to work with rupee currency and the methods of accountancy practised; he met and came to know well the Captains and Officers of the ships; he came in contact with all the Burmese and Indian clerical staff in the Head Office and with the principal shippers; and in the process of gaining this experience he impressed upon those with whom he was dealing the strength and integrity of his own character.

Large sums of cash were already beginning to pass through the Head Office and the benefits of George Swann's Glasgow training and of his first appointment as cashier for the Flotilla in Todd Findlay's Agency were reaping their rewards. By placing his British Assistants first "in the cash", as the newcomers' baptism became known, he established a practice which stood both the individual and the business in good stead during his own time and for generations to come. Making money is a main objective of any business. In the East it assumes a special importance in that, after it is made, securing its safe transmission in a widely spread operation requires sound methods of control and constant vigilance.

Kennedy next went over all the steamer services operated by the Company, travelling up to Mandalay and Bhamo and to Bassein and inspecting the Agencies. Within a year of his arrival he was fully competent in the performance of his duties as Assistant Manager and by 1880, when Swann was home on leave, it was decided that Kennedy should become Manager in full control in Burma and that Swann should be appointed General Manager, spending most of his time pursuing the Company's interests in U.K. and visiting Burma every cold weather season. But first Kennedy came home on leave in 1881 and was married in Falkirk in the summer of that year.

He did not take his wife to Burma when he returned from leave late in 1881; the country was too unsettled with the despotic rule of King Thebaw in Upper Burma and as it was there that Kennedy sought to open a new service on the Chindwin River, he had to spend much of his time up country.

The Chindwin is by far the greatest tributary of the Irrawaddy and, as we have already seen, the confluence of the two near Pakokku takes the form of a Chindwin delta, flowing into the Irrawaddy across an area over twenty miles wide. The impressive beauties of the Upper Irrawaddy defiles are not matched on the Chindwin, but as a whole in its navigable course of 400 miles it presents a grandeur of scenery which far surpasses the Irrawaddy.

There is no influence from the Himalayan snows on the waters of the Chindwin. Its source in the Patkai Hills, north of Assam, is one of the wettest places in the world, nearby Cherrapunji in Assam "boasting" perhaps the highest rainfall known of 450 inches a year. When the Chindwin rises as the south-west monsoon strikes that whole northern area it can become a veritable torrent, rising as much as thirty feet in one day. But this is exceptional and normally the high water season is a time of little trouble for the navigator — provided he knows the hazards, mainly in the shape of two notorious whirlpools. It is the season of low water which presents the problems for navigation and taxes the ingenuity of man.

Unlike the Upper Irrawaddy area, the banks of the Chindwin have always been well populated, large villages occurring quite frequently in the 200 miles between the principal town of Monywa and the old Upper Chindwin capital Kindat. The people are mainly Burmese, but in the upper reaches there are Shan enclaves and Nagas from the hills to the west. The climate is conducive to paddy cultivation, especially in the valley of the Myittha River which joins the Chindwin at Kalewa, and the traditional movement of the paddy for milling at Monywa is as fine an example of transportation economics as one could find. Rafts are built of the plentiful bamboo of the area, ten to twelve huts of dani leaves, better known as atap, are erected on the rafts and these are filled with paddy. With a tiny hut for the raftsmen, they are carried down the river and at their destination not only the paddy but also the rafts and huts are sold. In earlier days a canoe was carried for the return home of the raftsmen, but later even that was dispensed with in favour of a steamer ticket.

Early in 1881, accompanied by Annan Bryce, Manager of the British timber company, the Bombay Burmah Trading Corporation, Fred Kennedy had made a pioneering expedition up the Chindwin using one of the Flotilla Company's utility steam launches. Even at its draught of less than three feet laden with wood fuel and stores, this sixty foot single-deck screw steamer found problems of the low water Chindwin season to overcome.

Kennedy went to examine the possibilities for steamer traffic on the Chindwin and Bryce to inspect teak forests for which the Bombay Burmah Corporation had secured leases in the Upper Chindwin District. The fact that these representatives of two British Companies were permitted to travel into this remote part of King Thebaw's domain demonstrates that the royal mind was at least not closed to encouraging any exploitation by the foreigner which would result in revenues for his depleted treasury. The forest leases would be lucrative for the royal coffers and a steamer service would develop trade to their ultimate benefit also.

Meeting at Pakokku early in January, 1881, Kennedy and

Bryce, each with their parties of camp followers (for Bryce planned a longer tour intending to make a lengthy examination of the forests), set off on the launch for their pioneering journey. Problems of navigation were encountered as soon as they entered the Chindwin, the river flowing in shallow channels through its delta. Access from the Irrawaddy was only possible by a centuries old cutting dug for a royal progress, which had soon silted up, but was re-opened by nature in 1834 when an enormous flood came down, scouring out the old canal as a permanent channel. Only approaching Monywa, 70 miles from the Irrawaddy, the defined banks of the river began to be seen.

In the cool winter climate, marred only by early morning mists which can persist for two to three hours after daybreak, it could have been an idyllic journey. But there were frequent groundings and the subsequent delays of lightening and the laying out of anchors with all hands at the capstan heaving, the single screw threshing in the sandy bottom, made progress slow.

Annan Bryce recorded an amusing experience when the party were at Kin, a large village 130 miles up river from Pakokku, on the west bank. Behind the village he discovered a vast "jeel" or lagoon of water left by the inundation of the river in the high water season and this considerable expanse of water was covered with geese and duck of countless varieties. Great numbers of these birds frequent the Burma rivers during the winter and return to their summer quarters in Tibet across the Himalayas as the hot weather approaches. Fresh food was a problem for the party, particularly as the Buddhist will not take life (although catching fish has a special dispensation from this strict rule) and meat of any sort was unobtainable. Unaware that the King had given charge of the wild birds on this lagoon to the monks of the neighbouring monastery, Bryce secured boats and "made an excellent bag, none the worse for the immunity the birds had hitherto enjoyed". But while they were on the water they heard shouts and after landing they were asked to go to the monastery as the head monk wished to punish them for killing his birds by pounding them with his elbow. To receive this punishment the culprit is laid face down on the ground while his chastiser squats beside him with his arm doubled and makes a succession of sharp digs with his elbow into the soft parts of the back below the ribs. This could be very painful, and even dangerous, and in Bryce's own words "would have injured the prestige of our country for its first travellers to submit to even ecclesiastical chastisement, so under the whole circumstances we respectfully declined the honour of an interview with His Eminence the Abbot."

The up river journey ended at Kindat, having taken almost three weeks for 260 miles. It would have been impossible for the launch to proceed further, so low was the river level, but in any event Kennedy decided that there was little prospect of worthwhile traffic above Kindat and that the first venture on this difficult river should be between there and Pakokku. Bryce was now in the territory of his forests and they parted, Kennedy returning down-river in his launch, Bryce to make the passage later in country boats.

Satisfied that the Chindwin could be mastered by the right type of steamer, Kennedy spent time on his downriver journey assuring himself that the all-important supply of suitable firewood in billets for steamer boilers was available along the whole length of river. There could be no placing of coal flats as was practised on the Irrawaddy and dependence on wood was absolute, with stations for re-fuelling at intervals of not more than thirty miles. This was the first answer to draught restrictions in the low water season, every inch of hull emersion possible had to be conserved to carry cargo and passengers.

On his return to Rangoon, Kennedy convinced Swann that special steamers must be built for the Chindwin and proceeded to develop his plans when on leave in Scotland later in 1881. The result was the building by Denny of the Flotilla Company's first sternwheeler, the *Kahbyoo,* 170 feet in length, with two decks and a flying bridge, boiler forward, engines aft for trim. She opened the first service between Pakokku and Kindat the following year and the result was encouraging enough for the service to be increased during the high water season by the use of two of the smaller Irrawaddy paddlers. But general unrest in Upper Burma, which spread in 1884 and 1885 to the usually peaceful Chindwin, resulted in the temporary withdrawal of the service.

In the early 1880's Kennedy also spent much time exploring the prospects for further services in the Irrawaddy delta. Entirely in British Burma this fertile and potentially prosperous area had considerable attraction and little in the way of draught problems. Twenty new single deck screw steamers of 60 to 140 feet in length for the delta were delivered during that decade, built by Dennys and Duncans, and to the service from Rangoon

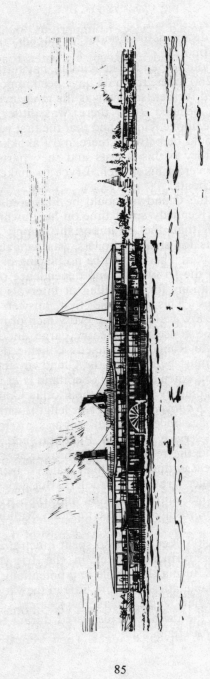

Early paddle steamers of the Irrawaddy Flotilla Company

to Bassein were added services to important population centres at Dedaye, Kyaiklat and Pyapon. Practically no means of transport existed in the delta except by water, roads other than within the townships being non-existent due to numerous creeks, large and small, which spread across the whole area. Paddy cultivation was on the increase, township and district courts had been set up and the prospects for a multitude of screw steamer services to replace the country boat and sampan were immense.

Extracts from Annual Reports of the Irrawaddy Flotilla Company:

1883 — "The Directors are glad to state that trade on the Irrawaddy has not been disturbed from any endeavour by the King of Burma to establish monopolies, though the unsettled political condition of Native Burma continues to hamper business with that country."

1884 — "The Directors, following the policy they have always sought to carry out, of doing everything in their power to develop the trade of the river Irrawaddy, determined to build two swift steamers to run between Rangoon and Mandalay, for the conveyance of passengers and the better paying type of merchandise. These are expected to commence operations towards the end of 1885."

These extracts demonstrate the determination which had already built up a fleet of thirty-nine steamers and sixty-five flats, a fleet being "kept in a state of thorough efficiency out of revenue". An Insurance Fund had been created, obviously a wise move with the high risk of casualties both from stranding on the capricious river and from the uncertainties of operating in King Thebaw's unsettled country. And most of the profits were being ploughed back into the business, a course on which the Board in Glasgow and the Management in Rangoon were firmly set.

The two "swift" steamers were *Mindoon* and *Yoma,* built by Dennys, and by far the largest paddlers yet commissioned, 310ft in length, 40ft beam and draught fully laden of six feet, but still in powerful trim at 4ft 6in draught. They were double-decked with the bridge on the lower deck, from where navigation was most favoured when towing flats alongside, and there was accommodation for twelve first class, twenty-four second class and around three thousand deck passengers. Fully laden they could carry 500 tons of cargo and tow a flat on each side with 600 tons in each, but this high water season capacity of 1700 tons could be reduced in low water by half. Like their predecessor the *Thooreah* they each had two funnels, not that this was necessary for practical purposes, but it was popular with the Burmese people and to this type of susceptibility the Company was only too ready to respond. The *Thooreah* had three decks and was 257ft in length; there had obviously been a considerable re-think in design since she had been built in 1880.

James Galbraith, that pioneering, venturesome spirit behind the foundation and success of the Flotilla Company, died in 1884 at the age of 66. He had never enjoyed robust health and in one of his early letters to John McColl in Rangoon, written from Harrogate, he complained of being there "for a few weeks in search of health of which I have been for some time rather short". He never visited Burma, confidently leaving the running of the business to Swann and Kennedy, in both of whom he had complete trust. His death was a milestone in the Company's history and coming as it did so close to the events of 1885 it marked the end of an era, an era conducted in the true style of the nineteenth century British merchant adventurers. And the impetus of his enterprise was to inspire those who followed, tremendous expansion taking place in the Company's activities almost non-stop for the next fifty years.

Peter Denny, already Chairman of the Flotilla Company, took over as Managing Director on Galbraith's death and carried on both offices for ten years, still remaining the leading figure in the Denny shipbuilding firm in Dumbarton. He maintained the progressive policies for the Flotilla which he and James Galbraith had adopted from the start, making an outstanding impact in these early formative years, an impact which others of the Denny family who were to follow him continued throughout the Company's existence.

CHAPTER NINE

PRELUDE TO ANNEXATION

They had been stirring times, these first twenty years since the Irrawaddy Flotilla had been handed over to private enterprise in 1865, and much had been achieved in the face of mounting problems in Upper Burma. Courage as well as foresight was required to maintain the steamer services and the momentum of the expansion on which the high morale of the staff depended. But the real excitement was still to come. Law and order in Thebaw's kingdom of Ava was declining and relations with British Burma continued to deteriorate; as 1884 drew to a close the growing anxiety felt by Fred Kennedy was transmitted to the Government of British Burma.

Kennedy wrote to the Chief Commissioner on 19th November:—

"I regret to inform you that, owing to the numerous and daring dacoities which have lately taken place in Upper Burma, a feeling of insecurity has sprung up amongst the commanders and crews of this Company's steamers when out of British territory, to such an extent that I have been earnestly asked to furnish them with arms as a means of defence. This I am unwilling to do, as it is possible in some instances they might be rashly used and lead to consequent misunderstanding; but taking into consideration the fact that the Irrawaddy Flotilla Company's vessels carry Her Majesty's mails, I think they are entitled to all moral protection that can be afforded them by the British Government, and would therefore seek that the subject may be alluded to in communications with the Court of Mandalay.

"As an instance of, and reason for, the feeling of insecurity prevailing in Upper Burma, the Governors of various towns in the districts have asked commanders to anchor their vessels in river under steam at nights, instead of following the usual course of mooring alongside the banks; and that within the last 10 days at Mymu, in the neighbourhood of Mandalay, a body of dacoits some 700 in number sent a defiant challenge to 1,000 King's troops who were in the vicinity to come out and fight. Such disturbances must have a depressing effect upon trade, besides a threatening one upon the lives of British subjects north of the frontier."

Again on 30th December, in response to queries on his first letter, Kennedy wrote:—

". . . at Sillaymyo, especially, by the Wun of the town himself, the commanders of various steamers were asked to remain in the stream and not moor alongside the bank at night-time in consequence of the disturbed state of the neighbourhood. This official was attacked in his court in broad daylight by dacoits and narrowly escaped with his life; and it was in consequence of this attack that he very considerately gave warning to the commanders of their possible danger. As the fact of acknowledging to Europeans that his district was at all disturbed might get him into serious trouble with the palace at Mandalay, I would ask for your reticence with regard to this official's name.

"Magwe was another district reported disturbed at the time I originally wrote and since then the Myothugyi of the town has been murdered by dacoits.

"The information about 700 dacoits challenging 1,000 King's troops at Mymu came from a Mr. Calogreedy, a resident of Mandalay, who was in the vicinity of Sagaing at the time the challenge was issued.

"I have only just returned from a visit to Mandalay, and though all the stations south of that city seem at present in a comparative state of repose, still it is impossible to tell when further outrages may occur, particularly as the late attack on Bhamo necessitates the removal of Burmese troops northwards, and consequently gives a fair field to the dacoits. To prevent such a contingency arising I would repeat the request contained in my letter of 19th ultimo, and ask the Chief Commissioner to lay such a statement of facts before the Ava Government as will serve to protect the lives and property of British subjects north of the frontier."

The Chief Commissioner then addressed the Minister for Foreign Affairs at Mandalay, expressing his fears that the trade between British Burma and the Kingdom of Ava would be seriously disrupted if the present state of insecurity continued. After making reference to the 'recent attack on the town of Bhamo and its capture by Chinese and Kachin rebels, resulting in the entire stoppage of trade between Mandalay and Bhamo', he asked, politely but firmly, that steps should be taken to restore law and order and that 'all possible measures be taken to protect from injury the lives and property of British subjects travelling or residing in His Majesty's dominions'.

The attack on Bhamo in November 1884 by Chinese and Kachin rebels was without doubt the result of unsettled conditions in the Ava kingdom. Emboldened by the general state of insecurity in the country, this large bandit group looted the town, made a rich haul and settled down in possession, driving refugees on to the wide sandbanks of the river, which was then at a low level. Fortunately for the refugees, the I.F. sternwheeler *Kahbyoo*, with her Danish born Captain Jan Terndrup in command, was approaching Bhamo at the time on the regular Mandalay/Bhamo service. *Khabyoo* had been withdrawn from the Chindwin and placed on the Bhamo Service for the low water season and with her ample deck space and a double-decked flat in tow, she had the capacity for such a rescue operation.

Captain Terndrup, although only 24 years of age at the time and a very junior Commander, was undaunted by the risks he had to take with his ship and her crew. He dropped his flat with his upward bound passengers well clear of the trouble area, and twice steamed up to the Bhamo sandbanks to take off the terrified refugees, amongst whom were European missionaries and traders and also Burmese whose homes had been destroyed by the fires of the raiders. Captain Terndrup took the Bhamo refugees to safety down the river and returned to Mandalay to make his report. The steamer service was suspended and remained so for many weeks until such time as the rebels withdrew from Bhamo; but in the meantime, as the year 1885 came and passed, other dangers grew for the ships and their crews at riverine stations along the route, of which more later.

Captain Jan Terndrup, who had joined the Flotilla in 1880,

was to serve the Company for close on fifty years, deciding as he approached the age of seventy that it was time to drop the anchor for the last time. He must have been a man of quite exceptional qualities to have retained the confidence of the Company in command on the precarious Irrawaddy for so long; everyone else, ashore and afloat, was retired at the age of 55, and usually they were ready for it by then. But this legend of a man was still there until 1929 recounting his experiences to a series of young officers who served with him; and one of these experiences, which was taking place about the same time as the Bhamo rescue, demonstrates the remarkable relationship which existed between Flotilla Commanders and the Royal House in Mandalay. Terndrup, being a handsome young bachelor with, in his own words, "a moustache like the Emperor or Russia", was often bidden to call on Thebaw's Queen Supayalat at the palace and claimed that he only stopped his visitations when he was aware that the King was becoming jealous of him; no doubt a prudent move.

There were other special relationships with the palace, including frequent visits by Captain and Mrs. Morgan, who had their home in Mandalay. Beyond the royal circle there was the Silk Shop in Mandalay of Madamoiselle Denigré, which had been opened by her French father before her, and which bore a proud signboard *Silk Mercer to the King and Queen of Burma and the Captains of the Steamers*.

It was, however, a young lady called Mattie Calogreedy, one of the family referred to by Kennedy in his letters to the Chief Commissioner, who was to occupy a key role in the drama about to unfold. The Calogreedy family were Greek merchants who had long been settled in Mandalay and had from time to time the royal favour. Mattie's mother was Burmese and her daughter was an attractive young woman in the early 1880s. She had married a Flotilla Company Captain whose name is obscure but who was given the unlikely alias of Captain Silas Bagshaw in a book which tells her full story. The Captain, however, died of a fever soon after they were married and it was the widow Mattie who played the part which contributed to the downfall of the Kingdom of Ava. Mattie became a Maid of Honour to Queen Supayalat and also her close confidante, resulting in her acquiring an intimate knowledge of life within the palace and of the perpetual intrigues which took place.

Meanwhile, with the departure of the British Resident, the

most important and influential foreigner in Mandalay was Cavaliere Giovanni Andreino, who was not only Agent for the Irrawaddy Flotilla Company but also for the Bombay Burmah Trading Corporation, the great British timber company which had concessions for the extraction of teak in several forests in Upper Burma. Added to these two prestigious appointments, Andreino was Italian Consul and it was in this position that he wielded the most influence with the King and his Ministers. A number of Italian adventurers had found a welcome awaiting them in the Ava kingdom, and more so since relations with the British had become strained, and now King Thebaw employed Italian mercenaries in his army, depending heavily on them to support his aggressive attitude towards British Burma.

King Thebaw and his Ministers had for some time also been encouraging French influence in Upper Burma when in June 1885 Frederic Haas was appointed French Consul and arrived in Mandalay. Haas had ambitions to bring off a diplomatic coup and oust the British influence once and for all from the Kingdom of Ava. With no British Resident in Mandalay, and despite the presence of a number of British merchants and of the Flotilla captains, the new French Consul had a clear field for his activities; or so it appeared, for he had failed to reckon sufficiently with the experienced Italian Consul. He proceeded with remarkable speed to acquire two far reaching concessions from the Ava Government for France, the first being approval for a plan to establish a French bank, which by arranging loans for commercial projects would soon gain a large measure of control over the economy of the country. The second was to build a railway from Mandalay to the British frontier at Toungoo; the effect of this on the British river steamers would have been serious, for a railway line had just been completed from Rangoon to Toungoo within British Burma.

Above all this, Monsieur Haas was pointing out to the Ava Government the advantages to be gained from a trade route to French Indo-China through the Shan States and the freedom this would secure from dependence on the ports of British Burma. Back in Europe, diplomatic exchanges on Burma between London and Paris had been taking place for a considerable time and everything Haas was planning was in breach of agreement reached between the British and French Governments on their respective positions in Upper Burma. The French were outwardly accepting that they would not interfere with this obviously British sphere of influence, while giving every indication to Burmese envoys in Paris that France was ready to help them. Haas' role was to administer the *coup de grace* to the British, who were unlikely to retaliate with force and risk a European war over Burma. He was to work with the utmost secrecy so that a *fait accompli* would be presented to the British administration in Lower Burma before they realised what was happening.

The eager M. Haas, however, was unaware that his Assistant Consul who had been in Mandalay for some years, had been carrying on an affair with Mattie. Monsieur Bonvillein, as he was appropriately named, had only recently returned from a visit to France with a wife, much to the consternation of Mattie, who immediately began to look for ways and means to get her own back. She had already established herself as a bearer of news from within the palace and had been a source of information to the outside world of another wave of mass killings ordered by the King the previous year, 1884. It was therefore with no little satisfaction that through a Burmese clerk in the employ of a Minister, who was her latest admirer, she acquired information on the French plans and proceeded to avenge her betrayal at the hands of the unfortunate Bonvillein.

Realising that the maximum damage to the French plans could be administered through Andreino, Mattie conveyed to the Italian Consul every detail she could obtain on the Haas proposals for the bank and the railway; and to this was added the equally explosive possibility that promises were being made for a fleet of French steamers to be brought to the Irrawaddy to run the Flotilla Company off the river. Andreino wasted no time in passing all this intelligence to the Company and to the Rangoon Government and shortly afterwards he was able to send evidence of French intentions to supply arms to the Burmese through Tonkin.

Confronted in London with these activities of the French Consul in Mandalay, the French Ambassador reported to his Government and obtained their complete denial of any such treachery in breach of their understandings with Britain on Burma. M. Haas was disavowed, but he was apparently not told so and continued his machinations. He had already taken upon himself also the role of adviser to King Thebaw on the affair of the Bombay Burmah Trading Corporation, which had begun earlier in 1885 before his arrival on the scene. The Bombay

Burmah was accused of evading the payment of the full royalties due on timber which had been extracted from the King's forests, and of failure to pay their just dues to their Burmese foresters. It was a trumped up charge following refusal by the Corporation to make a large loan to the spendthrift King. For over twenty years of working the forests there had been amicable relations and honourable fulfilment by the Bombay Burmah of their contractual obligations, all established on a firm footing during King Mindon's reign. But the Hlutdaw (Burma's State Council) held to their accusation when the whole matter was placed in the hands of the Chief Commissioner of British Burma, and in this they were encouraged by Haas.

Eventually, after further complaints to Paris, Haas was withdrawn from his post in Mandalay and ordered to go to Rangoon to await further instructions. Such a fall from grace could only be met by feigning illness, which he did and was gently conveyed down river on a Flotilla steamer. But the diplomatic damage was done.

The whole background of British relations with King Thebaw is contained in a minute prepared by Edward Sladen, by then Colonel Sladen, Commissioner of Arakan, in August 1885. Although rather out of the mainstream of these events, having been in his Arakan appointment since 1876, Sladen's opinion was sought and no one was better qualified to sum it all up. The extracts of his minute which follows demonstrate how patient and tolerant British policy towards Upper Burma had been in these ninety years since Captain Michael Symes had been despatched to the Ava Court.

Sladen wrote:—

"It is somewhat strange that our first political intercourse with the Burmese Court commenced (as it seems likely to end) with an attempt to frustrate French intrigue and a French occupation.

"Could we have foreseen all the troubles and complications which were to follow the occupation of Pegu in 1852, our best policy in the interests of the Burmese people and of our own Government would have been at that time to annexe the whole country, and to extinguish once and for all the Burmese dynasty. We were content, however, with our usual forbearance, to spare the dynasty, but rendered it effete and impotent for all the more serious purposes of war by occupying the whole coastline and leaving the Burmese no direct outlet by sea without passing through British territory.

"Amicable relations were maintained with the Burmese Court during the lifetime of 'the old King'; but the accession to the throne of King Thebaw was heralded in by wholesale cold-blooded massacres and by a studied disregard of his treaty obligations.

"History began to repeat itself with a vengeance. The dread of our power, which, in Lord Dalhousie's words, could alone secure peace, was surely fading away, as it had once done after the war of 1824. Our relations became strained. The treaty was a dead letter. Our officers, to use Lord Dalhousie's language, were again being 'worried away'. The attitude of the Court was so distant and even hostile that diplomatic intercourse could only be carried on at the capital under a serious apprehension of some gross outrage, which would of necessity result in war.

"By adopting this moderate and retiring course of action, we do not appear to have known that we were playing directly into Thebaw's hands. It was a grand deliverance to him to be rid of all possible interference and gave free rein to a headlong career of unlicensed despotism. The Government of India looked on at a distance, stern but unmoved to action. Inaction was misinterpreted or misunderstood. Our forebearance was put down to fear, and preparations were even made to attack British territory.

"The above remarks are prefatory only to the question which is to follow, and which is at present exercising the mind of Government, and of its loyal subjects throughout the whole country:— Have we still cause against Thebaw which justifies intervention and, if necessary, forcible interference.

"At the present moment our hand is being forced by the fact that the French have already established a political agency at Mandalay, and a French Consul now resides there for the purpose of representing French interests, though it is obvious to every one that no such interests (unless they are of a very remote or clandestine character) have any present existence in Upper Burmah.

"On the other hand, British interests, both in a political

and commercial sense, do exist, and are very closely allied to those of Upper Burmah. These interests are so jeopardized at the present moment that some immediate step is necessary to preserve the integrity of our dominions and protect British commerce.

"And not only are the interests of our own province seriously affected by anarchy and misrule in Upper Burmah, but the general interests of humanity are infringed by the continued excesses of a barbarous and despotic ruler.

"On all these grounds I contend that immediate active interference is indispensable for the purpose of (1) maintaining our political superiority, (2) of arresting grave complications which are imminent at the present moment, and (3) of securing good government in Upper Burmah.

"I maintain that these objects can only be successfully and permanently attained by annexing the whole of the country known as Upper Burmah. At the same time, I am well aware that Government will not resort to so final a step without first of all exhausting every other course of action, and being guided by results."

A change of Government in Britain in the autumn of 1885 brought about a dramatic change in attitude to the question of how King Thebaw's Burma should be dealt with. Lord Randolph Churchill became Secretary of State for India and was much more inclined to listen to the hawks than to the doves of the British administration in Burma and India and to pay more attention than before to the pleas of the commercial community for an end to the impossible conditions in which they were struggling to carry on trade. He was soon satisfied that firm action was required and convinced his colleagues in Lord Salisbury's Government that the Bombay Burmah affair was the last straw and that an ultimatum should be sent to Mandalay supported by the threat of military action if the conditions were not met.

CHAPTER TEN

FLOTILLA AT WAR

The closing months of 1885 brought no solution to the affair of the Bombay Burmah Corporation, nor any improvement in the relationship between King Thebaw and the Government of British Burma. In October Lord Randolph Churchill conveyed the decision of the London Government to the Viceroy of India that a clear ultimatum must be given to the Ava Government and that preparations should be put in hand to take military action should its terms not be accepted.

In Rangoon the Chief Commissioner of British Burma, Charles Bernard, wrote on 20th October to Fred Kennedy:—

"With reference to our conversation this morning, I write to ask you to arrange for keeping a steamer at Mandalay with banked fires, ready to bring away British subjects and European (and Eurasian) residents from Mandalay directly further stay there becomes unsafe. You, and we, leave it to Mr. Andreino to decide when he and the steamer shall come away. We must also leave it to him to decide how and when he shall warn other Europeans and British subjects. He should bring away the Post Office officials and cash with him.

"You can tell him that by the next steamer there will go a strongly and decidedly worded ultimatum, which will have to be accepted or rejected as it stands by the Ava Govt. after a few days deliberation. You can also tell him that preparations are being made for despatch of a large force from India. I have not yet heard if the Troops have started.

"From the time the steamer is kept with banked fires at Mandalay, until the time she reaches Prome with the refugees, she will be considered to be under engagement to the Government of India. But the usual fares should be levied from refugees who can pay, so as to prevent people coming away causelessly.

"The purport of this letter will have to be telegraphed to Mr. Ward* and I would ask you to caution Mr. Ward not to say a word on the matter to anybody, either before or after the departure of the steamer. It will induce greatly to the safety of Mr. Andreino and other Europeans up there if they get this preliminary warning.

"I would ask you and Jones ** to keep these matters to yourselves down here, as long as you can. Jones will use his discretion about warning or drawing away the servants of the Corporation in Upper Burma.

"You, Mr. Andreino, and others with whom he may communicate, will doubtless understand that private people are at liberty either to stay or come away as they like. The Government wishes to give them the fullest opportunity of coming away in safety. But the Govt. and the Public Treasury cannot be answerable for any money or trade losses which sudden departure from Mandalay may cause to refugees."

On the same day, Captain J. J. Cooper of the Rangoon/Mandalay Mail Service steamer *Ashley Eden,* at Rangoon ready to load for his next scheduled sailing, received an urgent message to report immediately at Head Office. There Kennedy told Captain Cooper that he had already seen Captain Matthews of the *Dowoon* and that *Dowoon* was bunkering in preparation for sailing at once single-handed for Mandalay to stand by ready to evacuate Europeans. For Captain Cooper there was an even more important assignment; he was to sail in two days time bearing the ultimatum to King Thebaw and was to deliver this crucial document to the Royal Palace personally, wait until 5th November with banked fires at Mandalay and then sail for Rangoon with or without the reply.

Both were dangerous commissions and the Captains, their officers and crews were given the opportunity to volunteer or stand down; every man on both steamers volunteered, British and Chittagonian alike. No Government official was to accompany them and the selection of a Flotilla commander to deliver the ultimatum document was said to have been quite deliberate. The Government of India were reluctant to send an official to Mandalay; the murder of the British Resident at Kabul was still fresh in their minds. Any risk of a further blow to

*Ward was an Assistant of the Flotilla Company in Upper Burma.
**Jones was Manager in Rangoon of The Bombay Burmah Trading Corporation.

British prestige could not be taken and it seemed that prestige would have been less offended had Captain Cooper been slaughtered in the course of delivering the ultimatum!

However, Captain Cooper survived. The *Ashley Eden* left Rangoon on 22nd October, called at Thayetmyo to report and arrived without incident at Mandalay on 29th, despite the fact that all the river marker buoys had been removed above the frontier. The Captain then proceeded to make his way to the Palace, three miles from the river, and duly delivered the document. Therein the Chief Commissioner of British Burma, on behalf of the Government of India, asked for a clear reply to several unconditional proposals, stating that, if these were not agreed, the British Government would "proceed to take such action as they may deem fit". The proposals required the Burmese King to receive an Envoy from the Viceroy of India with whom the dispute between the Burmese Government and the Bombay Burmah Corporation should be settled; that the Envoy should remain, be provided with a suitable residence near the river, permitted to have a British guard of honour and to retain a British steamer for his use. This diplomatic agent of the Viceroy was to assume control on behalf of the Government of India of Burma's external relations. Finally, the Ava Government were to grant "facilities for opening up communications with China via Bhamo".

This unequivocal ultimatum was quite deliberate and anything less stern would have been useless; any loophole for delay would have been seized upon and interminable negotiations would have ensued. Few in British Burma were optimistic that King Thebaw would acquiesce to such an abrogation of his independence, particularly as the ultimatum ended with a requirement that the Envoy of the Viceroy "should have free access to the King and not be asked to submit to any humiliating ceremonies inconsistent with the diplomatic usages of Western nations".

The *Dowoon* meantime had taken up station at Mandalay on 27th October and was joined by the *Rangoon,* the *Talifoo* and the *Shoaymyo;* these three Flotilla steamers had made safe passage in their normal trading to Mandalay. The two Mandalay / Bhamo service steamers, *Okpho* and *Palow,* continued the regular service to Bhamo, although their commanders, Captains Redman and Beckett, knew they could not be back in Mandalay before the *Ashley Eden* left with the reply to the ultimatum.

Shoaymyo left down from Mandalay before the arrival of the ultimatum and was safely reported at Thayetmyo on 1st November. The *Rangoon* left on 2nd November taking a number of European refugees who now thought better of staying on in the atmosphere of growing antagonism, everyone knowing that an ultimatum had been delivered and that war was likely; she also made safe and unmolested passage to Thayetmyo. So with the smaller paddlers *Okpho* and *Palow* still operating above Mandalay, the *Ashley Eden* waiting for the reply and the *Dowoon* and *Talifoo* standing by, the scene was set for what must have been one of the most important assignments in British Empire history to have been entrusted entirely to a commercial undertaking. All normal trading activities of the Flotilla Company above the frontier were suspended and only these five steamers and a number of flats remained in Upper Burma.

In Rangoon and in India the despatch of the ultimatum was followed immediately by preparations for the worst. British and Indian infantry and artillery regiments were put under orders to embark at Calcutta and Madras for Burma and a distinguished soldier, Major-General Sir Harry Prendergast, V.C., was appointed by the Viceroy, Lord Dufferin, to command the expeditionary force.

General Prendergast came from a family which had served the East India Company for a hundred years. Born in India in 1834, he won his V.C. in the Mutiny while serving with the Indian Cavalry, later transferred to the Madras Sappers and rose to Major-General shortly before being appointed in 1882 to command of the Burma Division. He had served in Burma for two years and was therefore familiar with the diplomatic and military problems which would face him when he received Lord Dufferin's call in October, 1885. The Viceroy warned him in a private letter that it was of course not yet certain that war would be declared on King Thebaw's Burma but that

"we must be prepared to strike at once in case Mandalay do not yield to our demands . . . but we must be careful not to despise our enemy too much . . . with this in view I have furnished you with a larger force than may perhaps be absolutely required. If your occupation of Upper Burma could be effected in a bloodless manner, it would be extremely creditable to you and far more advantageous to

the ultimate objects of the Government than any number
of victorious encounters in the field".

General Prendergast was also informed that his Political
Officer would be Colonel Edward Sladen, who had already been
released from his office of Commissioner of Arakan to be available for this key appointment. The choice was a wise one;
Sladen was as devoted to Burma and the Burmese as any British
official who had served in Burma, but he was under no illusions
as to the pitfalls of too much forbearance, as we have already
seen in his classic minute.

Prendergast's force of 10,000 soldiers, 7,000 camp followers,
500 mules and two mountain batteries of artillery, began to
arrive in Rangoon from Madras and Calcutta early in November. One British and two Indian Regiments, the first arrivals on
5th and 6th November, were transferred directly from their sea
transports to the Flotilla Company steamers *Thooreah* and
Alaungpyah. Some idea of the ability of these paddlers with their
flats to accommodate personnel on their spacious decks can be
gained from the number of Indian troops embarked by
Thooreah, which had three decks, and her two flats. This was no
less than 2,100 men. Preparations had already been put in hand
to prepare the steamers; a minute signed on 28th October by
Chief Commissioner Bernard recorded a meeting with the
Assistant Quartermaster-General:—

"IN THE MATTER OF TAKING UP FLOTILLA VESSELS

SETTLED — We must ask Mr. Kennedy to undertake the
fittings for us and to send us bills for the work on—

Arms racks.	Water-tanks.
Accoutrement pegs.	Cooking-places.

Latrines.

The sooner the work is begun the better.

I propose to take up each steamer and flat from the day
that the Commissariat begins loading it. This will,
probably, be about two days before the troops to go on
that steamer and flat are expected in the river.

The Port Officer will give Mr. Kennedy notice in writing
as each steamer and flat is taken up. And from the following morning loading will begin and the vessel will begin to

earn hire."

Kennedy had already been told that most of the Flotilla Company's fleet, which then comprised thirty-five steamers and sixty-three flats, plus a number of despatch launches, would be required to take the expeditionary force from Rangoon up river. In the event, twenty-six steamers, twenty-eight flats, seven barges and four steam launches were requisitioned and prepared for various duties, mainly as transports for troops, followers, mules and stores, but some for fighting purposes. The Indian Navy had appointed a Marine Transport Officer to be the liaison between the Company and the Burma Field Force, as General Prendergast's command was named, and this officer's day-to-day report of the whole campaign as it concerned the Flotilla Company's vessels involved, demonstrates and emphasises, if emphasis be needed, the vital part played by the river flotilla in the whole operation. The Times correspondent in Rangoon wrote that "the Company have unreservedly placed all their resources at the disposal of the Government and have subordinated all considerations of traffic to the paramount duty of carrying the troops".

But not only the Flotilla Company had rallied to the support of the British expedition. The Burma Field Force had no cavalry, due to the difficulty of transport from India, and according to the Times correspondent would have had no mounted unit had it not been for

"the spirited offer made by the mounted Company of the Rangoon Volunteer Rifles. This corps consists of gentlemen of good position and education and comprises many professional men and merchants. They provide their own horses and are fairly well drilled. Many of them speak Burmese and from their knowledge of the people will be well suited for outpost and reconnoitring duty."

Supplemented by mounted officers from regular infantry units of the Field Force and two British police superintendents, a small but useful cavalry unit was thus formed and added to General Prendergast's command.

Captain Cooper received the King's reply to the British ultimatum only on the last day permitted by his orders, 5th November; while he waited there was much consultation by

Ministers at the palace and no less rumour in the tense atmosphere in Mandalay. With the reply, the *Ashley Eden* made an uneventful passage down river, although deprived not only of the use of marker buoys, but also of the help of pilots; the Burmese Government had control of these above the frontier and had ordered their withdrawal. The long experience of Captain Cooper, and with his steamer unencumbered by flats, enabled him to make Prome in three days, night running being out of the question, and from there a British officer carried the reply by train to Rangoon, where it was received by the Chief Commissioner on 9th November. The message he telegraphed to the Viceroy amounted to refusal by the King to accept the main conditions of the ultimatum and the following day the Viceroy authorised that war be declared. A bizarre despatch was reported in the Glasgow Herald:—

"War has been declared against King Thebaw. No prospects of business this month. Prospects are good afterwards."

In the meantime, General Prendergast had arrived in Rangoon from Madras and, after consultation with Bernard, left with his staff by train for Prome. From there he was immediately conveyed by ferry steamer to Thayetmyo to join his command ship, one of the Flotilla Company's smaller but well appointed paddlers, the *Thambyadine*. Already the squadron of steamers and flats with their troops and stores were assembling at Thayetmyo and by 15th November the vanguard, comprising six Flotilla Company steamers and ten flats, also H.M. Indian Marine ships *Kathleen* and *Irrawaddy,* both side paddlers, were at the frontier ready to advance the following day.

The *Talifoo,* which had slipped her cable at Mandalay and escaped the forced detention to which she and the *Dowoon* had been subjected, had arrived at the frontier on 11th, having been detained at the Minhla Forts but again slipping away. Her Commander, Captain Ballantyne, brought useful information for the General. Those few Europeans who were determined to stay in Mandalay, headed by Andreino (who was in fact restrained from leaving, being held as a hostage for the Bombay Burmah Corporation) were now barricading themselves in the Flotilla Agent's house. Even before the declaration of war their lives were threatened, but now their chances of survival seemed

The fleet mustering for the advance on Mandalay

slim. More immediately of concern was Captain Ballantyne's report that two Italian mercenaries, Captain Comotto and Captain Molinari, were preparing to block the river at Minhla and that 8,000 Burmese troops were said to be encamped at the Kuligon Fort across the river from Minhla.

H.M.I.M.S. *Kathleen* and *Irrawaddy* steamed up the few miles across the frontier on 15th November to investigate these reports and were engaged in a short action with Burmese vessels which were being moved into position at Sinbaungwe to be sunk so as to block the channel. This they thwarted and all but captured the Italian Comotto, who jumped into the river and swam ashore. From papers which he abandoned it was clear that he had instructions to block the river at all costs, while Molinari was to ensure the invulnerability of the fortresses at Minhla and Kuligone. Taking the block, ships, a steamer and two flats, in tow, the two British gunboats withdrew to Thayetmyo and Colonel Sladen, who had instigated the sortie and had been on board the *Irrawaddy* was able to report to General Prendergast that a potentially serious delay to the expedition had been forestalled by the prompt and skilful action of the naval commanders.

While these preparations for the advance on Mandalay were proceeding, the *Dowoon,* and the *Okpho* and *Palow* in the upper river above the capital, were not forgotten and were the cause of much concern to the Flotilla Company, both in Rangoon and Glasgow. Despite the widespread belief that the reply to the ultimatum was unsatisfactory and that war was likely, Captain Redman had left Mandalay with the *Okpho* for Bhamo on 9th November, the day before the declaration of war, meeting up with the *Palow* downward bound late that same day. He anchored and signalled Captain Beckett and the two commanders held a brief consultation. Captain Redman suggested to Captain Beckett that he should not go alongside at Mandalay that evening on arrival, but lie off at anchor in case the expected declaration of war should come; and if it did he should proceed as fast as safety would permit for the frontier. The *Okpho* would carry on with her voyage to Bhamo and hope for the best.

Captain Beckett anchored *Palow* that night above Mandalay, summoning his three European officers (Chief Engineer, First Officer and Second Engineer) to his cabin. Plans were made for night watches and orders given for banked fires to be maintained ready for steam at short notice. In the morning the Burmese clerk would go ashore for the latest news.

When the Captain was aroused during the night to receive a Burmese visitor from the nearby river-bank, he was not altogether surprised, knowing his man well, to find Andreino, disguised in Burmese clothes, on board. Andreino brought news that the declaration of war was expected in the morning and that *Palow* should proceed down past Mandalay as soon as first light appeared. He also brought a Burmese flag and advised the Captain to present his ship as a Burmese prize, with the addition of the clerk prominently seated in the forward deck, dressed as a Wun (Government Official); and the necessary apparel for the disguise of the clerk was not forgotten by the resourceful Andreino. This ruse proved so successful that Captain Beckett made an uninterrupted passage to Thayetmyo, passing forts and batteries in full daylight and arriving at the frontier station in fading light on 11th November. The smaller and lighter draught *Palow* was able to make a smart two day passage which the large paddlers could not have risked. She came in shortly after *Talifoo,* which had been four days on the same journey.

Captain Redman was not to be so fortunate with the *Okpho.* Rumour was rife as this fine little paddler, built specially with the *Palow* for the difficult waters of the Bhamo run, proceeded up river with flat in tow carrying on her normal schedule. It was a week later, however, the day after General Prendergast's advance squadron crossed the frontier above Thayetmyo to assault the Burmese forts, before Captain Redman and his crew were made fully aware that Britain was at war with the King's Burma. At Moda, some sixty miles below Bhamo, a force of Burmese soldiers sent up from Mandalay met the *Okpho* and attacked her while the Captain and his three British officers were at breakfast. The ship was seized and the four officers were stripped to their trousers and ordered to walk over a single plank to the shore. As they were carefully keeping their balance on the plank, a volley was fired over their heads, but mercifully they made the shore, as there was a strong current running between the flat and the bank. They were then brought back on board, put in irons and forced into the forward hold where a gun was trained on them from the hatch.

The orders of the Burmese force were to make the Captain and his officers over to the local Wun, who was to execute them. This official, however, was a friend of the Captain, who had doctored his small son on the previous trip of *Okpho,* and he refused the order of the junior officer in charge of the soldiery, persuading him to escort the *Okpho* back to Mandalay. Her arrival at Mandalay Shore several days later at high noon in the full heat of the day resulted in a remarkable incident. There were no Flotilla ships at the ghaut, only two station flats which were there as permanent landing stages; even the *Dowoon,* which was to have been the "last-ditcher", was long gone. The Burmese soldiers dragged the British officers, still in leg-irons, on shore, hatless in the sun. But they had not reckoned with the Burmese waterfront workers who knew all the Flotilla men and were shamed by the treatment they were receiving. They surrounded the group of prisoners and escort, armed with bags of lime from a recent cargo, and compelled the soldiers to allow the prisoners to be seated in a bullock cart, giving them kamauks (wide bamboo hats) to shield their heads.

Thus they were taken to a Burmese gaol and their execution was prevented only by bribes sent to the Palace by Andreino through foreign maids-of-honour; and just in time came the final demand from General Prendergast for surrender and the promise that the lives of the King and his family would be spared if British subjects were found unharmed. Anticipating such a message, Andreino had also saved the lives of the few remaining Europeans in Mandalay, including his own, by sending warnings to the Palace through his intermediaries that when the British reached Mandalay, as surely they would, no mercy would be shown unless the Europeans were unscathed.

With preparations complete at Thayetmyo for the advance up river, the *Irrawaddy* and *Kathleen* leading the British squadron of transports, and with troops crowding the decks of the Flotilla steamers and flats, the vanguard of General Prendergast's Burma Force had left Thayetmyo and crossed the frontier on the morning of 16th November. The first incident was the appearance coming down river of a large steamer towing no fewer than four flats. The gunboats went forward to engage her, only to find that it was the *Dowoon,* for whom with the *Okpho* all hope had been abandoned. On seeing the British squadron, Captain Matthews anchored and General Prendergast ordered the *Thambyadine* alongside. When he and Sladen boarded *Dowoon* across her flats, there was ample evidence of damage from the shore batteries, the accommodation on the ship's upper decks being riddled by shell fire and rifle bullets, but none of any damage to the morale of the crew.

Captain Matthews had an exciting story to tell. He and his ship's company had given up all hope of being allowed to leave Mandalay, particularly after news of the declaration of war on the 10th had been received and the *Palow* had been seen passing down, apparently a prize to the Burmese. But on the following day a Minister came on board with a letter from his Government to the Chief Commissioner urging that the Flotilla Company steamers should resume their services "as their absence caused great distress in Mandalay". The staggering naivety of this move can only be attributed to the King's refusal to believe that the British were serious in their declaration of war. Captain Matthews was ordered to leave at once for Rangoon.

Ever mindful of Company property, Captain Matthews had the station flat to which he was tied up at Mandalay unmoored and taking her in tow proceeded downriver, picking up flats at Myingyan and Pakokku. At Yenangyaung he was attacked while taking his fourth flat in tow, a battery on the cliff promontory opening fire and inflicting damage to steamer and flats, but fortunately none below the water line. At Minhla, a number of Indian employees of the concessionaire of the Burmese Customs Post, British subjects, were seen to be signalling for the steamer to stop and pick them up, but when coming alongside to do so the Captain saw that Burmese soldiers were concealed in country boats at the ghaut. He immediately sheered off and rang for full speed, the crews on the flats repulsing an attempt to board. The batteries at Minhla and Kuligon then opened up but caused no severe damage, and that very morning another battery at Sinbaungwe tried to stop them with heavy salvoes. It was a miraculous escape, perhaps helped by poor gunnery, in some measure due to the protection to the steamer afforded by having two flats on each side, but mainly due to the courage and determination shown by Captain Matthews, Chief Engineer Macpherson, the other officers and Chittagonian crew. General Prendergast recorded the highest praise to them all in his despatches.

The day following this encounter, the advance squadron approached the forts at Minhla and began landing troops on both banks for the assault. Reinforcements arrived in six more Flotilla steamers with flats and on 18th further reinforcements of three steamers were brought up. One of these was the *Ashley Eden;* there was no respite offered to, or sought by, those who had been engaged in the preliminaries. The forts at Minhla and Kuligon were stormed and taken with little loss to the British force and the minimum necessary to the Burmese. There was gallantry, a British officer killed and another demonstration of great courage by Colonel Sladen who led one of the storming parties into the Kuligon Fort.

The action at the Minhla Forts was the only resistance of any real consequence, much reliance having been placed on their strategic position by the Mandalay Government. The Burma climate, however, made up for much of the weakness of the defences. While the Force was reforming in preparation for the advance up river, unseasonable heavy rain brought a sudden drop in temperature, putting many of the British troops out of action with tropical fevers. Outbreaks of cholera also occurred on several ships of the squadron; so virulent is this disease that immediate isolation is necessary and a troop flat was fitted up as a cholera hospital. During the advance no fewer than 270 cases were treated, resulting in over 150 deaths.

The *Dowoon* and sternwheeler *Kahbyoo* were in the last group of steamers to join the squadron, which was then complete, and the huge flotilla advanced on Mandalay; with *Kathleen* and *Irrawaddy* again in the van, the line of steamers extended for over two miles. Their first encounter on 18th November was the unexpected appearance on the bank of the river of two Europeans waving to attract attention. It was Comotto and Molinari, who had now decided to give themselves up. Papers taken on them revealed an elaborate scheme for the blocking of the river and that *Dowoon* had not been expected to be able to pass Minhla when she had been released from Mandalay. There was evidence also that other attempts at river blocking would be made at Pagan and at Ava, where there were forts on both banks guarding the approaches to Mandalay.

The only delays to the convoy in their advance occurred during short engagements at Pakokku and Myingyan, followed by the landing of garrisons. On 25th November they anchored at Yandabo, some fifty miles below Mandalay, where the Treaty ending the First Burmese War in 1826 had been signed. The next day a gilded royal barge came down river, pulling 44 oars and flying a white flag of truce. It brought a Burmese Minister with a letter begging for an armistice and declaring that the Burmese Government "have always had at heart the welfare of the English people and . . . have always protected the interests of the Irrawaddy Flotilla Company, the teak trade and ... of all British subjects". A request for cessation of all hostilities and the resumption of friendly relations concluded this hopeful communication. But there could be no armistice and General Prendergast, to whom the letter was personally presented, demanded surrender of the King, his army and Mandalay. He promised that "if his demands were accepted and the Europeans at Mandalay found alive and uninjured, the King's life would be spared and his family respected".

When no reply had been received by 27th morning the British squadron moved up to within striking distance of Ava, whereupon the emissary again appeared, this time with unconditional acceptance of the terms of surrender.

The vagaries of the Irrawaddy River were then well demonstrated as the squadron weighed to move up to Mandalay. Launches sent ahead to survey the river at Ava found that a Burmese steamer, several flats and small boats had been sunk in the main channel. After some hours of sounding, it was discovered that a new channel had scoured itself, assisted by the accumulation of sand behind the sunken craft, which had deflected the current of the river. The channel formed proved to be better in fact than the old one, hardly what the Burmese had in mind. With the forts at Ava and Sagaing invested, General Prendergast, now on board *Dowoon,* to which he had transferred his headquarters, continued his advance to Mandalay at daybreak on 28th November.

The squadron anchored off Mandalay during the morning, *Dowoon* and other steamers carrying troops going alongside the ghauts to disembark. The *Okpho* was there with a greatly relieved crew, including Captain Redman and his officers, who had been released at Andreino's instigation; they were much shaken by their ordeal and suffering from malnutrition and exhaustion. And Andreino was there to meet the steamers as they came alongside, accompanied by the few other Europeans who had remained in Mandalay throughout these critical weeks. It was to be his last act in the long drama, for the safety of his life was still at risk; in his various capacities he had contributed in no small measure to the downfall of the Kingdom of Ava and even with the die now cast, revenge could still be taken on him. He was given the protection of the squadron and relieved of his appointment as Flotilla Agent, Ward taking his place.

Three columns of the Burma Field Force were formed at the

Mandalay Shore to march by different routes to the palace. Sladen went ahead and was received by the King, while the guides for two of the columns were Captains Terndrup and Morgan, both of whom knew Mandalay well. The great enclosure of the Mandalay Fort, surrounded by its four walls each over one mile in length, was occupied and the following day General Prendergast took formal possession, proceeding to the Palace in the centre of the Fort. He was taken by Sladen to the King and after a short ceremony informed the King that he must immediately board a steamer with his family and go to Rangoon.

So Thebaw, last King of Burma, left his Palace in Mandalay with Supayalat, his Queen, and was conducted on board the Flotilla steamer *Thooreah* (Captain Patterson). They arrived in Rangoon on 10th December and were transferred to H.M.I.M.S. *Clive* to be taken to exile in India.

After the King's departure, General Prendergast ordered two expeditions to be prepared without delay, one for Bhamo, the other for the Chindwin. Six Flotilla steamers, including *Okpho, Palow* and *Kahbyoo,* with seven flats, took a strong force to Bhamo and three small steamers were despatched to the Chindwin. The General went himself with the Bhamo squadron, anxious to establish control over the northern area and to protect the frontier with China. Sladen was left in charge of the Hlutdaw in Mandalay to ensure continuity of Government, retaining for the time being the King's Ministers. Law and order in Upper Burma was bad enough already and the greatest problem now was to hold together some semblance of government, with the Burmese soldiery deserting in large numbers with their arms.

As the month of December passed there was growing speculation in Rangoon, Calcutta and London on what was to be done with Upper Burma. Was it to be annexation or should a suitable Prince be placed on the throne under a British Protectorate? At last, with the eventful year 1885 drawing to a close, the Viceroy received the British Government's decision that Upper Burma was to be annexed to the Crown and that proclamation to that effect was to be made on 1st January 1886.

By that time, with garrisons from the Burma Field Force established along the river from Minhla to Bhamo and on the Chindwin, the Flotilla steamers were returning to their usual employment, and trade in Upper Burma was resumed. It had not, in fact, been greatly disrupted except during those few weeks when the Flotilla was engaged with the expedition, but the resumption of operations had to be undertaken in the face of even more unsettled conditions than before.

Judging from the progress made in the years immediately following the annexation, however, the Company was undeterred. They were served by men of fortitude and of great determination, not forgetting also the skill of the steamer Captains, about whom the Marine Transport Officer of the Burma Field Force wrote in these somewhat phlegmatic terms on the part they played in the river expedition of 1885:—

"The difficulties of navigation were much enhanced owing to the disturbed state of the country having driven the pilots from their usual stations; but notwithstanding this I think I am right in stating that the movements of the fleet were conducted satisfactorily and reflected great credit on the Commanders."

CHAPTER ELEVEN

"NO SUCH RIVER FLEET IN THE WORLD"

Spending the summer of 1885 in Scotland, George Swann was kept advised by Fred Kennedy of the growing tension in Burma and in particular of the machinations of French Consul Haas in Mandalay. News from Andreino that the French were seeking even more concessions than those already known prompted Kennedy to telegraph to Swann late in September that:—

"French concession navigation River Irrawaddy likely to be granted. Bernard fully alive danger British interests and representing strongly to Viceroy urging immediate British interference."

This urgency in Rangoon drew little response from the Viceroy in Calcutta, nor from the Directors of the Flotilla Company in Glasgow, who decided that the matter could await the return of Swann to Rangoon in November. George Swann was on good terms with King Thebaw, to whom he paid his respects in person each time he visited Burma, and he was confident that he could turn the tables on the French. Even a month later, apparently having failed to grasp the seriousness of the increasingly troubled situation in Burma, Swann was writing to Kennedy with a list of gifts he was taking out to the King, including a £60 carpet and an equally expensive tea set, the whole list amounting to £250. "They will be shipped by the next Henderson Liner" he wrote "and will you please take good care of them until my arrival." And as a footnote he asked that Andreino should be in Rangoon when he arrived to give him an up-to-date report on the situation in Mandalay.

By the time Swann reached Rangoon, on 21st November, Andreino was in no position to do other than concentrate on saving his life and those of his European companions in Mandalay. Swann appears to have retained an optimism that yet again all would turn out well, based no doubt on his firm conviction that powerful Britain must continue to show a proper understanding of the strange ways of Burmese diplomacy.

Chairman Peter Denny wrote on 17th November from Glasgow to Kennedy:—

"Events have progressed rapidly these past two weeks and so far as my feelings are concerned satisfactorily. I am not hopeful of my views being shared by Mr. Swann from his intense sympathy with 'oppressed' peoples. Be that as it may, there appears little doubt now that Upper Burmah will be annexed giving us a time of quiet and prosperity in which we may hope that the 'oppressed' will participate. I am glad to learn that *Dowoon* has escaped and I hope to hear soon of the safety of *Okpho*. Mr. Swann will be sorry he is not on the spot."

Later, writing to Swann after the surrender of Mandalay, Peter Denny expressed the congratulations of the Directors to Kennedy and all concerned in the contribution made by the Company towards the speedy and satisfactory conclusion of hostilities. He then wrote, with the true roar of the mid-Victorian British lion:—

"I know that you are a Radical and some things else which I differ with you upon and also as to whether our country is an oppressor of nations and of such amiable monarchs as Thebaw. Anyway I am not going to be the bird to foul my own nest and I will leave this to foreign countries, John Bright and yourself. I am satisfied with your value as a friend and as an able counsellor in our business, so we shall agree to disagree on outside affairs."

The Viceroy, Lord Dufferin, paid a visit to Burma in February, 1886, by which time much water had flowed down the Irrawaddy and not a little blood with it. He was accompanied by General Sir Frederick (later Field Marshall Lord) Roberts, newly appointed Commander-in-Chief India, and one result of their on-the-spot examination of the disturbed state of Upper Burma was an immediate increase in the strength of the Burma Field Force, which eventually rose to some 25,000 men. But they also had to deal with serious personal problems affecting the two central figures in the capture of Mandalay.

General Prendergast and Edward Sladen came in for harsh criticism from different directions and for differing reasons; both were to be relieved in March and to leave Burma for good.

The Chief Commissioner, now *Sir* Charles Bernard, had followed the expedition to Mandalay to take formal control of the civil administration — he was now Chief Commissioner for the whole of Burma — and found himself at complete variance with Sladen on the policy to be adopted for the government of Upper Burma. Sladen strongly advocated a policy of retaining the King's Ministers, the Hlutdaw, with a British Commissioner effectively in control but receiving their advice. Bernard would not accept this, dismissed the Ministers and as soon as he had the Viceroy's ear saw to it that Sladen was replaced.

Nevertheless, in a speech on his arrival in Rangoon the Viceroy made special mention of "Colonel Sladen to whose courage and knowledge of the people we are so much indebted for the surrender of the King." His indebtedness was duly translated into a recommendation to the Queen that Sladen should receive a knighthood. So Sir Edward Sladen, after over thirty years service in Burma, retired to England and to continued controversy over his policies. Had they not been rejected, Upper Burma might well have been more settled after the annexation.

Lord Dufferin and General Roberts, with their staffs, travelled up and down the river between the railway terminus at Prome and Mandalay by the new Flotilla steamer *Mindoon*. They were accompanied by George Swann and a further expression of India's gratitude, this time to the Irrawaddy Flotilla Company, was shown by the bestowal of the honour of Companion of the Indian Empire (CIE) on both Swann and Kennedy. The appreciation of the Company was expressed in the Annual Report of the Directors for 1885, which referred to

"the energy and intelligent manner in which all members of the staff, including Mr. Stark the able Superintendent of the Dockyard, carried out the exceptional transport services required in connexion with the expedition to Upper Burma, which deserves the highest praise."

They also regretted the loss by foundering during the expedition of the steamer *Shwoay-la-Young* and the flat *Ava*, for which they were apparently carrying the risk themselves, as the losses were charged to Insurance Account.

Besides resuming the normal services which had been conducted before the war, the Flotilla Company fleet was strained in 1886 to its limits by increasing demands from Government for trooping. Newly arrived units from India had to be taken up river, the relieved brought down and movements from district to district carried out to enable the army fulfil its role of pacification.

En route from Glasgow to Rangoon in November that year, George Swann went to Calcutta and purchased three powerful steamers and six flats from the India General Navigation Company, whose services on the rivers of Bengal required similar shallow draught vessels. They were safely steamed down to Rangoon from Calcutta in December and went straight into service. The cost was £100,000.

But this was only a stop-gap and a vigorous 3 year programme of building was embarked upon. The fleet of 1886 consisted of 40 paddle steamers and 64 flats; by 1888 it had grown to 65 steamers and 101 flats and in addition there were 17 creek steamers for delta and ferry services. In these three years capital expenditure exceeded £1 million, then a tidy sum. The Directors told the shareholders that "there is now no such river fleet in the world."

They also had to tell them, however, that the state-owned railway had opened a line from Rangoon to Mandalay; and between these terminals was the largest part of the Company's business. For the remainder of the Flotilla Company's existence there was intense competition for traffic, not only to and from the Prome and Mandalay railheads, but also in areas in the fertile dry zone east of the Irrawaddy where, between river and rail, large crops of cotton and pulses were grown.

The new additions to the fleet included five sternwheelers for the Chindwin, where attention was again turned as conditions became more settled. Yarrow, then of London, now the well known Clyde shipbuilders, received their first order for a stern-wheeler in 1886 and many were to follow. Like Denny, Yarrow specialised in the light steel hulls of shallow draught so necessary for the Burma rivers.

The years of prosperity and growth suffered a setback in the early 1890s when poor prices for Burma's paddy crop brought depressed trading conditions. India was in trouble too and a severe drop in the exchange rate effectively devalued the rupee, which stood at 1/6d in 1890, to 1/3½d in 1893, and it was to be some years before it recovered to stabilise at 1/6d again. The effect in Burma was severe, especially for the British working there who had dependants at home. It brought to the Directors of the I.F. Company a memorial signed by 37 Commanders, complaining that they were being harshly treated when they were asked to accept a cut in pay as well. But the depression was widespread and the Flotilla men had to accept the lean years with everyone else.

1894 saw changes in the leadership of the Irrawaddy Flotilla, both in Glasgow and in Burma. In failing health, Peter Denny handed over that year as Managing Director to John Innes, a Henderson partner, and when Denny died a year later he was succeeded as Chairman by James Clark, a member of the Paisley thread manufacturing Company.

George Swann retired in 1894 to Colintraive in the Kyles of Bute, where he had found a peaceful retreat after a strenuous business life, a life devoted to Burma and her people and to the now great Company which he had played such a large part in creating. He was an uncompromising Burmaphile, but still severe with any transgressors of his high standards of integrity. Always the elegant bachelor, he was affectionately known in the Henderson office in Glasgow as Gorgeous George and liked and respected by all. The systems of cash safeguards which he introduced, not only at the Rangoon Head Office but also on the steamers and at the Agencies throughout the country, stood the test of time, remaining substantially unchanged throughout the life of the Company. He was only 56 when he died in 1896.

Frederick Kennedy took over as General Manager of the Flotilla Company in 1894 on Swann's retiral and lost no time in persuading the new Chairman and Managing Director that an even faster rate of growth in the Company's activities could be achieved despite the depressed trading conditions of the time. But first he took John Innes over the whole system in the winter of 1894/95 and the Managing Director's report when he returned to Glasgow pointed to the opportunities for the future. He wrote:—

"On my arrival at Rangoon on 15th December last I found business generally at a low ebb. On every side complaints were heard as to the impoverished state of the country owing to the low price ruling for paddy during 1893/94.

Accompanied by Mr. Kennedy I visited all the leading branches of our business, leaving Rangoon by rail to Mandalay, thence by steamer to Bhamo, and Bhamo to Rangoon by river, touching at all the intermediate ports. I also visited the proposed tramway route from the Irrawaddy to the Chindwin, spent several days at Bassein and at Moulmein . . .

On the upper Irrawaddy and Chindwin there is a fleet of some forty Government steamers, launches and flats, mostly small craft, carrying commissariat stores and troops. They do not cater for public passengers or cargo, but we suspect the crews make a slight addition to their income by carrying passengers on the quiet. Those I passed on the way carried little cargo and few passengers, but with such a fleet the work performed during the year must be considerable . . . There is no comparison between the Government fleet and our own, even military officers avoiding Government craft when they can and travelling by ours . . .

From the Chief Commissioner we get but little sympathy or consideration, his recent policy being to cut down our allowances for mail and other contracts . . . he is fully posted regarding our Company and our pleading the stringent situation with the payment of a 10% dividend at home is not quite consistent in his eyes . . . He tells us that Calcutta drains his revenue to the utmost, leaving him little for public works in Burma . . .

Further developments are continually before Mr. Kennedy . . . From Bhamo to Myitkyina we run a small steamer during low water, under Government concession, but on completion of the Mu Valley railway to Myitkyina this concession may no longer be obtainable. It is a trifling matter so far as we are concerned but without the concession we could not make ends meet . . .

The object of the Irrawaddy/Chindwin tramway is to avoid the difficult shoal navigation between Pakokku and Monywa . . . and our steamers could start up river with much larger cargoes than they take from Pakokku. The tramway would carry the traffic from Myinmu on the Irrawaddy to Monywa. To test the matter thoroughly we have two of our Captains (on half pay) taking statistics of the cross traffic during three months and this should help us in coming to a decision.

Dalla Dockyard is held under lease from Government and at close of the lease in 1898 we may have competition for the renewal, but we have the adjacent property at Kamakasit available for workshops and dock if necessary. Dalla returns are helped by revenue from docking and painting of sailing ships in the South American white rice trade, but this trade is drifting into steamers and without it an outsider could do little good at Dalla. A large amount of repair work is also obtained from rice mills and from steam launches in the harbour. Dalla workshops are in first rate order and we have generally 400/600 men at work . . .

Mandalay slipway and workshops are under lease from Government until 1906. Repairs to our own fleet, local repairing work and sawing of timber keep the yard employed at a fair profit . . .

Of our properties the head office in Phayre Street, Rangoon, is one of the finest blocks in the city and the Manager's house, Belmont, has been one of the best residential houses in past days. The Belmont compound of some ten acres is a capital piece of ground; its proximity to the centre of Rangoon may render it valuable by and bye. Mandalay Agency House and Office should be written down in value. Bassein, Bhamo, Pakokku, Prome and other properties are all in good order . . .

In going over our various lines I was particularly struck with the first class manner in which our steamers are kept up, due in great part to Mr. Kennedy's continual personal supervision and his close knowledge of technical details. Next to the style of our steamers is the superior type of our Captains and I had this opinion confirmed by conversations with Rangoon friends. To this is no doubt due the almost complete immunity from accidents which we experience.

The friendly relations between Mr. Kennedy and all our staff was also quite evident . . . On the upper river we were accompanied by Mr. Purdie, our Agent at Mandalay and his knowledge of Burmese was of the greatest service. To Mr. Findlay, Mr. Hay and Mr. Wilkinson of our Rangoon staff I am also greatly indebted for the many details they compiled to assist me.

With a slight turn for the better in trade there is plenty of work both for the Railway and our Flotilla, in a country like Burma capable, with increased population, of very great trade expansion in the near future. I am sanguine that the *Irrawaddy Flotilla Company* will hold its position as a dividend paying concern, in spite of the erratic rupee.

Surprise has often been expressed by tourists travelling in our steamers that the Irrawaddy is not better known. For beauty of scenery nothing could surpass the defiles of the river above Mandalay and for interest the daily round of sights on the lower river between Rangoon and Mandalay."

Ranging as it does over the whole field of the Company's operations and future problems as he saw them in 1895, this report by John Innes demonstrates just how much courage was required to commit large capital sums to expansion at that time. The Directors were persuaded, however, that they must be ready for an increase in trade, and consequently of public travel, if they were to maintain their near monopoly; and Kennedy was convinced that prosperity for Burma was not far away. In the event, he was right and the decision then to build for the future was perhaps the most important that the Company ever took.

Some of the problems touched on by John Innes in his report were soon resolved. Before the turn of the century the Government decided to discontinue their commissariat steamer services on the upper Irrawaddy and Chindwin. The railway to Myitkyina was opened and the concession to run between Bhamo and Myitkyina enjoyed by the Flotilla was withdrawn, but the trade was of little consequence and this was no great loss.

The proposed tramway from Myinmu on the Irrawaddy to Monywa on the Chindwin never materialised. Later the Railway opened a line from Sagaing to Monywa which achieved the same purpose — and in 1931 a rail bridge was built across the Irrawaddy from Ava to Sagaing. The Chindwin river services developed mainly from Monywa, but through services from Pakokku, which was the Irrawaddy/Chindwin transhipment centre, were continued despite the severe low water season problems of the Chindwin delta. The Chindwin trade prospered and a service was opened to Homalin, 140 miles beyond Kindat and 400 miles from Pakokku.

The Irrawaddy delta, with the population growing rapidly as

Thambyadine, General Prendergast's command ship for the advance on Mandalay, 1885

Paddy raft on the Chindwin

Officers of the *Japan* at Mandalay 1906 prior to embarkation of the Prince and Princess of Wales (later King George V and Queen Mary)

Oil towing paddle steamer leaving Yenangyaung with two loaded flats

I. F. & Airways seaplane delivering mails to *Mysore* for Viceroy of India (the Marquess of Linlithgow) en route Prome to Mandalay, 1937

Mysore steaming into Mandalay with Viceroy, 1937

A three-year-old elephant coming ashore from a flat — reluctantly

Rangoon/Bassein Express twin screw steamer *Waikato*, 115 feet in length

the acreage under cultivation for rice paddy expanded, was now ready for a network of steamer services. The Flotilla Company introduced a fleet of double-decked twin-screw creek steamers, from 90 to 115 feet in length, licensed to carry from 250 to 500 passengers. This fleet grew in numbers to more than one hundred units as the delta developed over the next twenty-five years. At the peak in 1908 sixteen new 90ft creek steamers were added to the fleet in one year and by then the whole delta from Rangoon across to Bassein was being served, with many of the services based on the larger townships such as Bassein, Henzada, Yandoon, Myaungmya, Bogale and as far up river as Prome. From Rangoon alone there were more than twenty sailings daily to delta destinations.

At the same time a fleet of steel cargo barges (C.Bs) was built up to handle paddy from delta buying stations to rice mills and rice from the mills for direct loading at the ports to ocean ships. Tugs which could tow up to eight C.B.s at a time and steam barges with towing capability provided the motive power for the C.B. fleet, which eventually grew to number some two hundred units. After much trial and error to meet the requirements of the rice trade, the size of C.B. was standardised at 90 feet length with capacity for 120 tons rice or 5000 baskets of paddy.

The lease at Dalla was renewed and in due course the land was purchased outright, the dockyard modernised, houses built for the British staff and quarters for the large number of Indian workmen. Dalla Dockyard grew with the fleet and eventually employed some 3000 men. Another establishment at Ahlone on the Rangoon side of the river was acquired in 1904. This was the Rangoon Foundry, where slipways were built for the creek steamers and repair and engineering work were carried out, employing 1500 men. Here also artesian wells produced ample quantities of water for the fleet and for water barge services to ocean going ships in Rangoon harbour.

The Kamakasit property adjacent to Dalla was retained and became a coal storage depot where cargoes of 8/10,000 tons were landed from Calcutta by C.B.s for distribution to the fleet.

The slip and workshops at Mandalay became Mandalay Dockyard, the land was purchased from the Government and a house built for the British Superintendent.

The Chief Commissioner's words to John Innes that Burma had her revenues "drained to the utmost" by the Indian Government were the evidence, if any evidence was still required, why Burma remained an appendage of India. The office of Chief Commissioner of Burma was upgraded to Lieutenant-Governor in 1897 and a Legislative Assembly was created, but only limited effective participation in their affairs was given to the Burmese people until the Act of Separation from India in 1937.

As we have seen, by the turn of the century the ramifications of the Company were enormous, yet they continued to grow. The spirit of enterprise never waned in the men who followed Swann and Kennedy and there was no lack of support from the successors in Glasgow of Galbraith and Denny. John Innes proved to be an outstandingly successful leader of both the Henderson business, where he was Senior Partner for over thirty years, and of the Flotilla Company Board; he remained Managing Director until 1927 and was Chairman from 1924 until his death in 1929.

But there is still much to tell of Fred Kennedy, and of the expansion to which he committed himself and the fortunes of the Flotilla while he was General Manager from 1894 until 1906; and he was to be involved for another ten years after that as a Director of the Company in Glasgow.

Carriage of crude oil from the central Burma oilfields became an important traffic after the formation of the Burmah Oil Company in 1886. Soon the original refinery at Duneedaw in Rangoon became too small for the increasing volume of oil being won and operations were moved to Syriam, where once again this prime location for water-borne trade was exploited. Special tank flats were built by the I.F. for the oil traffic and special oil flat towing steamers, side paddlers, with extra tall funnels to reduce the fire risk. This was mainly a one way traffic from the oilfields down river to the refinery, but frequently oil well materials were loaded direct from ocean ships to the decks of the oil flats in Rangoon for delivery upcountry.

But it was not long before the Flotilla Company were to receive a rude shock and threat to their lucrative oil business. John Innes was a director of the Burmah Oil Company — the head office was in Glasgow as it still is today — and heard the news in 1901 with dismay that the possibility of a pipeline from the fields to Rangoon was being examined. He was in Burma again that year and it appears that he had a stormy meeting with David Sime Cargill, founder and Chairman of Burmah Oil, on his return. Kennedy had reported that the project was thought to be feasible and was deeply concerned at the prospect of laying up his oil fleet, which he had steadily been building during the past five years.

Innes failed to persuade Cargill not to proceed and the pipeline was completed in 1908. Then fortune smiled on the Flotilla Company, for in that same year the great British trading Company of Steel Brothers entered the oil business, forming the Indo-Burma Petroleum Company. Their introduction to the trade was the result of a joint partnership with a successfully established Indian oil well owner who found himself short of capital. This was followed by the building of a refinery at Seikkyi, a few miles down the Rangoon River from the city. The oil fleet thus gradually regained its employment, another British oil company also setting up in business and both using the river route for their crude oil.

In 1898 Kennedy had turned his attention to the three rivers at Moulmein, on which steamer services were being operated by an enterprising Englishman named Dawson. Dawson had four double-decked creek steamers and had also built an eight mile stretch of $2\frac{1}{2}$ feet guage railway from Thaton to Duyinzeik and a workshop and slipway at Moulmein. Kennedy bought the lot for the I.F. Company and continued running the railway until the state Railway opened a line from Rangoon to Moulmein only a few years later. He expanded the creek services on the Moulmein rivers and ran a ferry service across the Salween from Martaban to Moulmein.

The Moulmein steamer services proved to be quite unprofitable to the Flotilla Company with competition from the Indian owned Burma Steam Launch Company, which persisted far beyond Kennedy's time. Frequent attempts to buy out this troublesome opposition were in vain, but in 1920 they were at last persuaded to sell and nine more creek steamers were added to the I.F. fleet. With a monopoly on the three rivers which converged on Moulmein and well equipped dockyard services, this self-contained little fleet became a viable arm of the Company's operations.

Kennedy was also much involved in the design and building at Denny's for the Flotilla of the largest shallow draught river side-paddle steamers ever to exist anywhere in the world. Seven double-decked paddlers of the *Siam* class were delivered and re-erected at Dalla Dockyard between 1903 and 1909 and were to remain the last word for the Express Service between

Twentieth century Flotilla steamers at Rangoon

Rangoon and Mandalay until 1942. They were 326 feet in length, 46 feet in beam and drew six feet fully laden. Their power from triple expansion engines enabled them to tow two flats each of 250 feet in length and lift close on 2000 tons in steamer and flats at maximum draught. The customary two funnels of the earlier large paddlers gave way to a single funnel, both for practical reasons of design and for the benefit of the overall appearance of the new type vessels. The Burmese riverine population, quite dismayed at first at this departure from the traditional two funnels and the loss of power which only one funnel seemed to imply, soon came to accept the graceful lines of these magnificent ships. Their spacious decks were licensed to carry 4200 deck passengers and the well appointed first class accommodation for 16 on the forward upper deck and for 24 second class aft provided every comfort for the many tourists and business travellers.

Towing their two laden flats, one at each side, these great paddlers carried sufficient power to make the six hundred miles passage in the low water season between Rangoon and Mandalay in five days. The opening of the Twante Canal, a short 22 miles cut which joined the Rangoon River directly to the main stream of the Irrawaddy, eventually reduced the passage by some 100 miles as compared with the long Bassein Creek route and restored the distance to be steamed to that of the old original Panhlaing Creek route. But equally important to the Express Service which the paddlers conducted was the introduction of a night Commander to relieve the Captains between Magwe and Chauk, where channels permitted safe running at night with searchlights. And by dropping one flat at Pakokku (for Chindwin traffic) and the other at Myingyan, the steamer going on to Mandalay single-handed and picking up her flats on the down river passage, the round trip Rangoon to Mandalay and back was completed in twelve days.

Frederick Kennedy, obviously an innovator of the take-over technique as well as an outstanding manager, died at his home in Edinburgh in April, 1916 at the age of 68. His wife, who had spent many years with him in Burma, survived him for another sixteen years, herself one of the pioneers — British women who accepted the discomforts of the Eastern climate supporting husbands in their work and such as Kennedy in the position which he held for so long. They had no children and were thus at least spared the family separations which bore so heavily on the lives of those who worked "East of Suez".

The Flotilla comprised some 200 units when Kennedy took over full control from Swann in 1894. When he died in 1916 the number exceeded 500, which included close on 200 powered vessels, from the great *Siam* class paddlers to the minute buoying launches, and 320 flats and C.B.s. This immense fleet employed more than 5000 men, mostly their Chittagonian deck and engine crews and with a further 5000 employed at the four dockyards, plus the Head Office and Agencies' staffs, not to mention some 200 British Officers, Engineers and Assistants, the total payroll exceeded 11,000. The familiar red-banded black funnels of the Irrawaddy Flotilla had become a permanent part of the Burma scene.

CHAPTER TWELVE

DARKENING SHADOWS

The reader has had but a cursory account of these thirty years of the Irrawaddy Flotilla when the greatest growth of the fleet took place in the unified Burma. In that period there were no great world events to bear well or ill on progress, which went ahead with only minor interruptions as the economy of Burma expanded.

But while the First World War of 1914-18 affected Burma only indirectly, overseas trade being restricted by lack of ocean shipping, it drew heavily on the resources of the Flotilla Company, both in men and in ships. Some of the British staff left to join the Forces and no less than 89 vessels of the fleet were requisitioned by the British Government for the Mesopotamia campaign along the River Tigris. And orders for new ships were held up, with British shipyards fully engaged in building for the Navy and the merchant fleet.

The Flotilla's shallow draught steamers and flats were ideal for the Tigris and the first to go were seven of the medium sized paddlers, which were sent over to the Persian Gulf under their own power soon after the declaration of war on Turkey in November, 1914. They were first well boarded up to protect their open decks and limited freeboard for the ocean passage, but the *Shweli,* a newly built 230 feet paddler for the Bhamo run, broke her back and foundered off Ceylon. The remainder, which included sternwheelers, tugs, buoying launches, flats and barges, were towed across by ocean-going tugs and ships and all but one arrived safely; a sternwheeler capsized in the Bay of Bengal and was lost.

British deck and engine officers and Chittagonian crews of the Flotilla went with this fleet to Mesopotamia, all volunteers, enlisting in the Inland Water Transport Corps of the Royal Engineers. There were casualties, mainly from the climate in "Mespot" which took a heavy toll of life in that campaign, but at the end of hostilities all the Flotilla men who had survived the rigours of the unhealthy summer humidity and scorching heat in the Shatt al Arab returned to their civilian jobs in Burma. Not so most of the Company vessels, which had been literally run to death.

The war over, the Company settled down to replacing their fleet losses and bringing their number of British staff up to full strength again. Then the fleet began to grow once more as trade developed in that post-war era. The 1920s brought the peak of prosperity to Burma and at the end of the decade the fleet of the Irrawaddy Flotilla numbered 622 units — 267 powered vessels and 355 flats and barges. By then they were carrying annually some nine million passengers and $1\frac{1}{4}$ million tons of cargo. And although the fleet was to grow in number to 650 in 1941, in terms of capacity it was at its peak in the 1920s and had become the greatest inland water transport enterprise the world has ever known. No doubt there was, and still is, a much greater volume of traffic moving on the Mississippi, and possibly elsewhere, but we know of no other single commercial operator or fleet of this size.

When economic depression hit the world in 1930 the effect on Burma was severe. The price of paddy fell to and remained at a low level and the order of the day everywhere was retrenchment or at the best standstill. Unemployment brought a wave of anti-Indian feeling amongst sections of the Burmese, especially in Rangoon where Indian labour was predominant. When Indian workers in the port went on strike in 1930, Burmese were brought in, broke the strike and then saw the Indians returning to the jobs which they would have been ready to continue, despite their traditional disdain for labouring employment. This sparked off riots between Burmese, who roamed the city attacking Indians, and Indians who retaliated. Many of both communities were killed and strong Government action was required to bring the situation under control.

Of even more concern to the Flotilla was the outbreak of a rebellion in Central Burma the following year, led by a formidable nationalist called Saya San who incited several thousand of his countrymen to join him in his anti-foreigner movement. They were ill-armed, but created immense problems of security when the rebellion spread to the delta and only firm action by the Government and the help of army reinforcements from India quelled the uprising. But for over a year, and long after Saya San had been captured, there existed this state of localised rebellion.

Flotilla Company Assistants, constantly on tour in the delta, were armed during the period of the emergency and travelled in pairs. These necessary precautions highlighted the exceptional conditions at that time, for in ordinary circumstances an Assistant would be out in the delta on inspection tour for several weeks at a time alone, with only his *lugale* (Burmese servant), and unarmed.

Also in 1931 there was further rioting in Rangoon, this time spreading to upcountry towns, against the Chinese community, yet another symptom of anti-foreign feeling asserting itself, provoked by the economic situation. The suppression of the rebellion in 1932 signalled a period of quieter conditions, which an apparent beginning to economic recovery in 1934 helped to sustain. There was, however, little impetus to these signs of recovery and in the following years political unrest was fomented on a depressed economy, with small but effective groups spreading anti-British propaganda throughout the country. Yet there were few open signs of hostility to the British community and certainly none to the men of the Flotilla Company. In 1937, after a peaceful acceptance of the principle of separation from India, Burma finally cast off the yoke of being a small part of that great Empire and became its own Commonwealth country, with a Secretary of State in the British Government.

Separation from India, however, did not mean an exodus of the large Indian population, by then established in Burma for over 100 years, and more than a million in number in a total population of sixteen million. They constituted an essential part of almost every British enterprise in the country, were still employed in large numbers by the Government and were the backbone of the labour force in Rangoon and the other seaports at Bassein and Moulmein. We have seen that the Chittagonian from Bengal was by far the largest group in the Flotilla, all Mohammedans; and that the smaller number of Hindu clerks and durwans were also important to the smooth functioning of the Company. Many feared the growth of anti-Indian feeling, but few even thought of leaving Burma despite another wave of rioting, and attacks on Indians in particular, in 1938. It was yet another sign of the build-up of nationalist and racial agitation.

Despite these unsettled 1930s, the Flotilla Company forged ahead. In a static economy there was little room for expansion of steamer services, but the formation of a subsidiary Company, Irrawaddy Flotilla and Airways Limited, saw them take to the air, one of the first shipping Companies in the world to see the potential of the aeroplane as an alternative to water transport. At the same time, 1934, they purchased as a going concern the small Pazundaung Foundry on the creek of that name close to Rangoon, where a hangar for aircraft was built and the "hard" into the water adapted for seaplanes to be wheeled up and down on cradles.

I. F. & Airways was a bold venture, founded largely on the Agency which the Flotilla Company had secured for Imperial Airways, forerunner of B.O.A.C., and now British Airways, when the Empire route was extended from Calcutta to Rangoon, Singapore and Hong Kong in 1933. By then the flying-boat route to the Far East was being planned and "water-borne" Agents were appointed — the Flotilla Company in Rangoon, Mansfield and Company in Singapore and Jardine Matheson in Hong Kong. This link with British aviation enabled the Flotilla to engage on secondment Imperial Airways' pilots and engineers for their first seaplane, a Fox Moth, and for the three Short Scion eight-seater seaplanes which followed. Services were operated to Mandalay via the oilfields and down the Tenasserim coast to Moulmein, Tavoy and Mergui.

But a parsimonious Government gave no encouragement to Burma's first airline; no mail contracts were forthcoming. And in the 1930s people were not sufficiently air-minded, nor had they the money, to support air services, and the project was abandoned in 1938, a decision accelerated by the loss of two aircraft. One was destroyed by fire and the other while alighting on the water of the Inle Lake, high in the mountains of the Shan States, fortunately in both cases with no loss of life.

In 1937 the Bhamo route into China came on the scene again. The mule caravans were still there on the trail to Tengyueh, but the new development was for the transport of an entire aircraft factory from Rangoon to Bhamo, whence it would be taken overland across the frontier into Chinese territory at Loiwing for erection. Kenneth Gourlie, the youngest and most junior Assistant in the Flotilla, received a lengthy telegram from his brother Dan, who was employed by the Curtis-Wright Aircraft Corporation in America, enquiring as to the capability of the Irrawaddy Flotilla to receive ex ship at Rangoon and carry to Bhamo "a factory for making aeroplanes". It seemed a tall order, but when Gourlie handed over his telegram to the Traffic Manager he was promptly given an affirmative reply to despatch to his brother. In due course the factory was built at Loiwing in Yunnan, but sad to relate it was bombed by the Japanese before production was in full swing and the remains were dismantled and re-shipped down river.

This was not by any means the only result of the Sino-Japanese War, which had closed all the ports of China's eastern seaboard, for it brought through Rangoon a flow of traffic for China. From Rangoon it went by river to Bhamo and into Yunnan, and later in even greater volume by the road built from the Shan States railhead at Lashio into south-western Yunnan. The years 1937 to 1939 therefore saw Burma actively involved with Britain and America in supporting China, but observing a frail neutrality with Japan. This continued through the British declaration of war on Nazi Germany in September, 1939 and until Japan entered the Second World War in December, 1941. The seat of Chiang Kai-shek's Government of China had been withdrawn to Chunking, and Kunming, the capital of Yunnan, had become a centre more vital to China than ever before. Burma had assumed world importance with a vengeance and for almost a decade from 1937 was to remain a strategic area of war and its aftermath and to suffer untold misery in two campaigns between the British and her allies, and the Japanese.

Little wonder that radical political elements in Burma exploited the British involvement in the war and were ready to co-operate with the Japanese both before and after they invaded Burma from Thailand in December, 1941. The British-controlled Government of Burma suffered the humiliation of being unable to summon sufficient forces of support to stop the whole country being overrun by the Japanese armies by May, 1942. We shall now see how the part played by the Irrawaddy Flotilla in the longest retreat in British military history far surpassed all the earlier exploits which have so far been recounted.

CHAPTER THIRTEEN

JAPANESE INVASION

When John Morton became Manager of the Irrawaddy Flotilla Company in January, 1941, he was the eleventh to hold that office. Of the eight Managers who followed Swann and Kennedy there has been no mention — and little more than a synopsis of the years when they were guiding the Company on its successful course. That success is the best tribute which can be paid to them all.

Morton did not take the typical route to an appointment in the Flotilla Company. This was via employment in the Glasgow offices of Patrick Henderson & Company, where the young aspirant was well watched for three or four years before being offered the much sought after appointment of an Assistant. John Morton was not one of these Henderson apprentices, but he was the son of a notable father who was a well known Bailie in the City of Glasgow and no doubt received the necessary and well chosen introductions. John was 22 years of age when he was appointed an Assistant and sailed for Burma in 1912.

During the thirty years of his service with the Flotilla, John Morton acquired an exceptionally high level of perception both of the country and of the esprit de corps within the Company. He was something of an extrovert, spoke his mind and knew how to enjoy life while keeping within the bounds of propriety required of him as an Assistant in the I.F.

His pride in the fleet and in the service was shared by the British staff ashore and afloat, among whom there existed a spirit of comradeship which also spread in its effects throughout the whole organisation; to the Burmese who filled the clerical posts at the offices up and down the river, many as Agents and some in later days as Assistants; to the Chittagonian watermen who came in their thousands to man the fleet; to others from India of many Hindu castes from senior clerks to the lowly sweepers; and to the small but valuable number of Anglo-Burmese, many of whom were in important Agencies after being

132

apprenticed as supercargoes and inspectors on the steamers.

Morton wrote his first Annual Report as Manager to the Directors in Glasgow early in 1941. He was reviewing the year 1940 and expressed concern at that critical time during the war with Hitler for the safety of all at home, including the Directors. This sentiment was one which in the past had come frequently from Glasgow, the Directors being concerned when times were troubled in Burma for the safety of the British staff. For the time being the roles were reversed, but only for a very short time and John Morton was not unaware of the growing danger of the war spreading to the Far East. His report went on:—

"Burma is technically a belligerent but has hitherto escaped the physical ordeal of war. Now, due to Japan's ambitions in the East, hostilities have come appreciably nearer to her borders and there is apprehension in informed quarters regarding events in Indo-China and Thailand. There is growing awareness in responsible Burmese circles of the dangers which threaten the country and a growing eagerness to help the war effort, which was unfortunately absent before. This is reflected in the vernacular Press and in the steady progress now being made in raising additional units for the Services in Burma.

"We have at present nineteen of our covenanted (British) staff serving with His Majesty's Forces. Three Office Assistants are on full time active service, also four Deck and three Engineer Officers, while three Assistants and seven Officers are undergoing militia training at Maymyo."

1941 was a tense year in Burma. Apprehension as to the intentions of the Japanese grew and preparations went ahead for the worst. Everyone who could be spared from British Companies and the civil administration was called up and new units continued to be raised. The calls of the campaign in the Middle East had reduced India's forces to a minimum and little help could be expected from there; in fact it became evident that little help could be expected from anywhere for Burma and Malaya, so heavily committed was Britain in Europe and the Middle East.

In Rangoon it became a case of "waiting for the balloon to go up" and in a lighter vein the event coincided with a portent for the more superstitious of the local population. A Henderson

Liner arrived in Rangoon early in December with a barrage balloon aloft, the first to be seen in Burma — and a few days later on 7th December the Japanese struck at Pearl Harbour. When the British battleships *Repulse* and *Prince of Wales* were sunk off the Malayan coast three days later, Burma knew that dark days lay ahead.

The Japanese had overrun Northern Malaya and Thailand and were at Burma's Tennasserim frontier in two weeks and at the same time they hit Rangoon with devastating air raids, devastating not so much on property as on people. In the first of these, with the streets of the city crowded in mid-morning, anti-personnel bombs took some 2000 lives. The waterfront area suffered most, many Indian coolies being killed when Japanese aircraft dropped their vicious bombs amongst them as they scattered for shelter. In the panic which followed, most of the population fled from the city, some to return later but many of the Indian community in particular deciding there and then that Burma was no place in which to remain.

This was the scene at Christmas 1941, a city in disarray, a country demoralised and the Japanese invader already threatening Moulmein. The Flotilla Company had their first casualties in the air raids on Rangoon. Standing on the bridge of the Mandalay Express steamer *Nepaul,* Captain George Ferns and Chief Engineer Watt were killed by a bomb which fell on the foreshore close to where the steamer was moored. The whole waterfront area, extending for some two miles and including the wharves for ocean going vessels, became in an instant a shambles with so many dead that it took several days to remove the bodies and to restore some order.

Rangoon gradually began to function again as a city, but when Moulmein fell at the end of January, 1942, and there was little sign of reinforcements to stop the inevitable advance on the capital, more and more Indians left for the safety of Bengal, some by the ships which came and went from the port, some by road or rail to Prome, whence they crossed the Irrawaddy and trekked across the Arakan Yomas. The Flotilla Company steamers were crowded by others wanting only to leave Rangoon and seek shelter with friends or relatives in the delta or upcountry, or to join the trek from Prome.

The entire fleet of the Irrawaddy Flotilla had by then been formally requisitioned by the Governor of Burma. However, apart from the small number of the British staff who had been called up to the Services (some of whom were later to be seconded back to keep the Flotilla going) the ships and establishments continued to be run with the Company's employees remaining civilians. John Morton stayed in control, but he was now responsible to the Army Commander.

The battle for Moulmein brought the first brush by the Flotilla with the enemy, if it may be called that, as the steamers and men were armed with no more than an occasional Lea-Enfield rifle. One of the Moulmein passenger steamers on the Gyaing River was machine-gunned from aircraft and a number of the Chittagonian crew killed. She was then bombed and sunk with further loss of life. When the Army withdrawal from Moulmein was ordered, the Company's Marine Superintendent, Captain John Reid, went to Martaban, sought out sufficient men of the Chittagonian crews, who had by that time left their ships for the safety of shelter ashore, manned five steamers and brought them across the Gulf of Martaban to Rangoon. The remainder of the Moulmein fleet were scuttled in the first act of denial by the Flotilla Company, a denial to the enemy which was to develop in the next few months into the wholesale scuttling of practically the entire fleet.

The British force could not defend Martaban after the loss of Moulmein and soon fell back first to the Bilin River and then to the Sittang River. If the Sittang could not be held Rangoon would be wide open to the Japanese Army, which already had two strong divisions on the ground in Burma, far outnumbering the British. The time had come for the evacuation to the safety of India of British wives and children and for the Flotilla Company to move the local Head Office staff out of Rangoon with their families. Morton put Assistant Manager Roy Dry in charge of this latter operation, and having embarked his large party on one of the steamers, Dry set off up river for Mandalay with such Company records and equipment as could be hastily gathered together. It was then early in February.

Singapore fell to the Japanese on 15th February and it was no surprise when the official order for the evacuation of Rangoon was given on 20th February. The Sittang could not be held for more than a few days and preparations were now being made to destroy or immobilise the oil refineries and other installations in the Rangoon area in a massive act of denial. In two or three days the enemy could be at Pegu and Rangoon soon encircled.

Those of the population of Rangoon of some half a million

who had remained in the city, and there could still have been 100,000, now besieged the railway and the river steamers and in 24 hours the city was deserted. All but the last-ditchers, mainly British employees of the oil, timber and rice milling Companies ready for the final denials, had gone. The Flotilla had their part to play and John Morton selected a small group of Assistants and Superintendents who left their homes and gathered at the head office building in Phayre Street, there to live an improvised existence for whatever time remained. The Dockyard Superintendents prepared to immobilise their plant, the Marine and Engineer Superintendents to organise storing and manning of the steamers, flats and barges as they were despatched up river. An Assistant went off by fast launch to cross the delta and order creek steamers based on Bassein and other outstations to make for Henzada, and the remainder set to, endeavouring to control the refugees who clamoured to embark on the steamers as they left Rangoon. This little group were then assigned their various parts in the final preparations. Some were to stand by with two double-decked creek steamers ready to take all the demolition parties from the mills and refineries to their escape by ocean going ships already held at anchor further down the Rangoon River, others to remain with tugs and keep the Chittagonian crews at work.

As the steamers were despatched up river, many flats and C.B.s with valuable cargoes of rice and Army stores went with them, leaving behind some thirty C.B.s with bunker coal for the fleet and with ammunition, bombs etc., still awaiting orders. There were flats too, requiring a powerful tug to move them and Captain John Gillison, in command of one of the Flotilla's largest tugs, *Kamakyi,* began towing them through the Twante Canal to the main Irrawaddy, clear of the immediate danger. The same process began also with the coal and ammunition C.Bs, two smaller tugs with ever watchful Assistants on board working night and day to remove as many as possible from Rangoon harbour. Each return into Rangoon from the Canal anticipated a possible quick about-turn in case the Japanese might have arrived, the surest signal that they had not being continuous fires rising above the city. Looting and arson were widespread, mainly the work of the inmates of the Rangoon jail, who had been released on evacuation day and became the only other inhabitants with the last-ditchers.

Several eerie and uncertain days passed. The Sittang Bridge

was blown on 22nd February in a disastrous but gallant withdrawal, which spelt the beginning of the end of effective British resistance. Now there seemed nothing to stop the Japanese marching into Rangoon. But there was to be a temporary respite; and hopes were raised by the arrival in Rangoon in sea transports of 48 Armoured Brigade, comprising the 7th Hussars with their tanks and two battalions of British infantry. Army Headquarters remained at Rangoon and on 1st March Lieutenant-General Sir Harold Alexander flew in to take over command. It was a last desperate effort to save Burma, but even the future Field-Marshall could not perform miracles — and he all but ended his participation in the war in the dramatic days which followed.

For the Flotilla last-ditchers the time gained enabled them to clear Rangoon of all their craft and despatch the ammunition barges upriver to Prome. How much they would have preferred to have taken many of the steamers out to sea — a risky but not impossible proposition at that time of year — and round to Akyab or to Calcutta. But the official dictum was that Upper Burma was to be held and John Morton was ordered to keep the fleet in the river.

Not until 7th March had the Japanese overrun Pegu and were pushing down the road to Rangoon. They were then astride the road junction 14 miles north of the capital and had cut off British Army headquarters, who were at the Mingaladon cantonment on the northern outskirts of the city. General Alexander was as good as "in the bag". But so eager for the prize of Rangoon were the Japanese that their 14th mile road block was abandoned to concentrate an encircling move on the capital; Alexander and his staff, with elements of 48 Armoured Brigade, wasted no time in making their escape northwards to join the main British force.

That same day the demolitions were carried out, the men involved were collected by the two Flotilla creek steamers and all were safely ferried out to the last ocean going ships held for their escape to Calcutta. The dockyard establishments were immobilised by their own Superintendents, who then had to take part in the next sad duty of scuttling the two creek steamers.

Also on that eventful 7th of March Captain Gillison in *Kamakyi* was anchored off Syriam awaiting orders. When he learned of the road block, and that the Twante Canal and much of the delta was in the hands of Burmese elements supporting the

Japanese, he decided to seek out the Naval Commodore at the shipping anchorage down river. As he left Syriam the first explosions in the demolitions of the refineries heralded the imminent arrival of the enemy and as he steamed down the Rangoon River smoke and flames surged into the skies.

Gillison not only found the Commodore but also two other Flotilla Captains, both in their uniform of officers in the Burma Navy. Lieutenant-Commander Richard Spears was on duty in command of *Weeno*, an I. F. Company double-decked creek steamer under requisition to the Navy, and Lieutenant Alastair Campbell of M.L.1103 of the Burma Navy. Spears, a great-grandson of Thomas Spears, whom we first met at Amarapoora in 1852, had joined the I. F. Company in 1932 with a sea-going Master's Certificate and by 1939 had risen to a senior command on the Mandalay/Bhamo Express Service. He was one of those released by the Flotilla for service in the Burma R.N.V.R., where he had earned quick promotion.

The order issued by the Commodore, Burma Coast, to Lieutenant-Commander Spears speaks for itself:—

"You are to take the following vessels under your command — *Panhlaing, Kamakyi* and *M.L. 1103* — and do your best to reach Akyab. Report progress at 0800 daily — convoy will be in easy range of you."

Panhlaing, commanded by Lieutenant Robert Love B.R.N.V.R., another I. F. Company Captain, was the Flotilla's largest tug and already requisitioned by the Navy; and she was then known to be making for Rangoon from Akyab.

Thus began, in the grim two months that followed, the only incident with a happy and satisfactory ending for the Irrawaddy Flotilla. Apart from *Weeno, Kamakyi* and *Panhlaing*, the entire fleet was trapped in the Irrawaddy and Chindwin.

Spears left with his command that night in company with the convoy taking out the demolition parties, but the next day had to drop behind when they ran into heavy weather, *Weeno* in particular being in difficulty. With Campbell navigating from the well equipped *M.L.*, and *Kamakyi* in close attendance to *Weeno* and hugging the coast, they made the shelter of the Bassein River at daybreak on 9th March and proceeded to Diamond Island where they were joined by Love with *Panhlaing*. The weather moderated the next day and the little flotilla steamed on up the coast and reached Akyab safely on 13th March.

All this while the main drama was being played out on the Irrawaddy. John Morton was on the river that D day, 7th March, deploying his resources in British staff, including the remaining last-ditchers who were out of Rangoon and clear of the delta just in time. It was now a full scale military operation on the river and after a brief re-forming at Henzada, the fleet from the delta and Rangoon began to assemble at Prome. There for a further two weeks a hectic disposal of some 400 steamers and barges upriver was carried out, at the same time despatching military stores, rice and other foodstuffs from a massive accumulation at the Prome railhead.

Morton was now in Mandalay, directing the river operation and in close contact with the Army Commander. He had placed British Assistants at Prome, now the key forward position for defence of the Irrawaddy valley; at Magwe, where a hastily enlarged airfield provided a base for the R.A.F.; at Yenangyaung to ensure movements of oil and petrol; and at Monywa to prepare for an influx of paddlers from the Irrawaddy if the enemy could be held in lower Burma until the first rise of the Chindwin in May. With Morton in Mandalay were his Marine and Engineering Superintendents, Assistant Manager Dry and three senior Assistants, while up and down the river the British Captains and Engineers were sustaining the whole operation. But they could not be on more than a limited number of the 250 steamers, let alone the barges, and it fell to the senior Chittagonian masters on the smaller paddlers and other steamers to show an example to the already extremely frightened crews. The Chittagonians are not a martial race; it might even be said that they are the very opposite and they had little stomach for a meeting with the advancing and now dreaded Japanese. Nor were they helped by the sight of thousands of refugees making for safety while they were expected to remain on their ships. They were still civilians — and they were only too aware of it — and maintaining their flagging morale became a vital part of the operation.

Any river man reading this account may wonder how creek steamers and others, built for the deeper waters of the delta to draughts of over five feet in light condition, could navigate the Irrawaddy in that extreme low water month of March. Little was heaven-sent for the Flotilla at that time, but when the daily guage telegram from Bhamo told those in Prome that a rise in the river was on its way, this was news of that sort. In the event it was all futile in terms of saving the ships — they merely had to be scuttled further up river — but for the movement of supplies it was vital. It was a brief rise lasting only a few days, but the Flotilla men knew how to use it.

When the Japanese Air Force blasted the R.A.F. out of Magwe in mid-March, achieving surprise strikes on aircraft on the ground, the river and the Prome base in particular were left unprotected. The Jap was constantly overhead, bombing and straffing. Even the restriction of movements on the river to hours of darkness, with the moon dimly showing the channel marks, only reduced the frequency of attack from the air. Searchlights had to be abandoned. And as casualties grew, Chittagonian morale fell to a low ebb. Yet this did not apply to all crews, for Captain William Rea, the quiet but tough senior tugmaster of the Flotilla, had volunteered to take over command of the double-decked creek steamer *Hastings* for a hazardous mission — and his crew agreed to go with him.

Hastings was detailed at Prome to take a raiding party of British and Australian Army officers and other ranks, led by a young Sapper Major, down river to Henzada, which was known to be in enemy hands. Most of the officers were instructors at a Bush Warfare School that had been established at Maymyo, near Mandalay, and this was their first chance of an engagement with the enemy. And a sharp engagement they had, suffering a number of casualties. Two of the *Hastings* crew were captured by the Japanese and one was killed. Captain Rea, who had been one of a small number of British Flotilla staff hastily commissioned into the Army a few days before for special duties, was later awarded the Military Cross for the courageous part he played in the raid. The Sapper Major was Michael Calvert, Commandant of the Bush Warfare School, soon to become a column commander and later a brigade commander in Wingate's Chindits.

Now two of the largest paddlers, *Siam* and *Mysore,* with Captains Chubb and Railston in command, had been converted to hospital ships. Hundreds of casualties from the fighting withdrawal up the Irrawaddy valley during these March weeks were taken up river first from Prome, then from Allanmyo and Yenangyaung. The Red Cross on their roofs was respected by the Japanese, which was a blessing, for their aircraft had complete control of the skies over the river, where the Flotilla were suffering heavy casualties. An example of the terrifying situation to which the men on the steamers and their passengers, military and civilian, were exposed was the assault in moonlight on the paddler *Sinkan*. Chittagonian Master Bassa Meah, with a heavy tow of two large flats and 4 C.Bs laden with ammunition, was navigating from his flying bridge as he approached Thayetmyo, when *Sinkan* was attacked by Japanese aircraft. He remained steadfastly on the bridge endeavouring to draw closer to a high river bank, but when bombs hit his ammunition barges he had to cast off the blazing tow. The heaviest casualties were among British and Indian troops, machine gunned by the low flying aircraft; and the survival of Bassa Meah and his helmsman something of a miracle.

Prome, and Toungoo on the main road and rail route to Mandalay, fell at the end of March as the Japanese pushed northwards, and soon the harassed Flotilla were helping to evacuate the oilfields. Much of the fleet was now at Mandalay, spread out on the long straight reach of the river there, many without crews, but with Morton and his little group using every resource available to keep supplies and troops moving. General Alexander sent him officer cadets and men from the Burma Auxiliary Force to assist in manning vessels which were now being selected to go on up river when Mandalay itself was threatened. And as that nightmare month of April drew to its close, no-one doubted that it was only a matter of time until not only Mandalay, but the whole of Burma would have to be abandoned. The dreaded but now inevitable preparation for the denial of a large part of the fleet at Mandalay was put in hand. Scuppering these lightly built steel hulls presented no great problem and they needed only to settle on the river bottom for the approaching seasonal rise of the Irrawaddy to deny them to the enemy. By the next low water season they would be well and truly silted up beyond salvage.

John Morton wrote in his diary on 28th April:—

"Mandalay was evacuated yesterday, the I. F. being the last to go. The Army is retreating up the Chindwin. Our men won't be many days at Monywa and I expect them to retire up river and so through to Manipur. Macnaughtan has been at Semeikon (below Mandalay) ferrying the Army across the Irrawaddy. I have a guarantee from General Slim that he and the crews of the steamers there will be taken safely to Monywa.

"We are being chased out even quicker now than was expected and I have orders for more sinkings here at Kyaukmyaung. There are over two hundred of our fleet sunk at Mandalay. Imagine how I felt drilling holes in their bottoms with a Bren gun."

Mandalay had been bombed almost flat by the time the evacuation had been ordered and casualties at the river were heavy. British engineers from the Burmah Oil Company and Government service who had volunteered to man crewless steamers were among a number killed on a raid at the steamer ghauts and Abdul Hakim, the most senior Chittagonian Master of the Flotilla, was also killed on his bridge.

Still at Kyaukmyaung Morton wrote on 30th April:—

"We have sunk more craft and the Army have sunk all the ammunition barges and flats we brought up with such labour. We are taking many thousand evacuees up to Katha. What has to become of them after arrival at Katha (and to us!)? The Japs have made such progress that there is doubt if the Tamu Road will be open — assuming we can get across to the Chindwin."

Moving with amazing speed through the Shan States, a Japanese force was in Bhamo as Morton's last ships steamed up to Katha on 3rd May. His attempts to warn the Bhamo Agent that all craft were to be scuttled had failed and it was there that several paddlers fell into enemy hands. The Agent, Captain Frank Musgrave, who had returned from retirement to take charge at Bhamo, managed to escape to Myitkyina from where he was flown out to Dibrughar in Assam. Unaware of the situation on the river between Mandalay and Bhamo or on the Chindwin, he believed that he was the only one of the British staff to have succeeded in making an escape. It was not an unreasonable conclusion; in fact the Flotilla men were the last to leave Katha and among the last to leave the Chindwin.

Morton's diary on 3rd May:—

"Katha is a sight, vessels anchored ten abreast and all deserted. The last train has gone, the town is evacuated. Parties are told off to sink every vessel, get our three cars

142

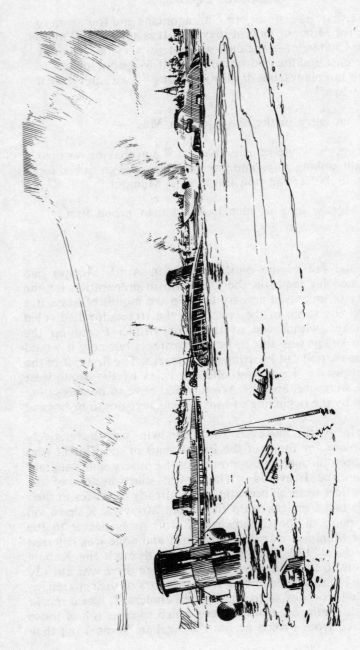

Denial to the Japanese invader

ashore first, pay off all our Chittagonians and free them to make for Manipur as best they can. It is at least 150 miles to the Chindwin — the cars will not get very far. The day is overcast and the rains are not far off. We want low cloud for the Jap planes, but dry for marching — we can't have it both ways."

The final entry in the diary for 4th May:—

"This morning we re-assembled at 4 a.m. having worked all night sinking ships and paying wages. We go to bed for one hour before starting the trek to Manipur."

John Morton and his men had lost their proud fleet.

After the fall of the oilfields early in April, Morton had strengthened his team on the Chindwin in preparation for the possibility of increased activity there in the month of May. But very soon the speed of the retreat up the Irrawaddy had ruled this out: the withdrawal of the main British Force up the Chindwin valley was still to be the strategy, but now it would have to be carried out by using jungle tracks. The first rise of the Chindwin was a long way off; the rains of the south-west monsoon were not, and the Army would have to be across the Chindwin by the beginning of May if they were not to be bogged down.

Early in April, however, the Chindwin was a relatively peaceful place for those of the British staff of the Flotilla who had just been through these months of the misery and slaughter of war on the Irrawaddy. The eleven sternwheelers of the Chindwin fleet were all operating, and already evacuees in their thousands had been taken up river from Monywa. Kalewa, on the west bank of the Chindwin and 150 miles nearer to the frontier of Manipur, was their objective; and none was deterred by the trek of 100 miles from Kalewa through the Kabaw Valley, notorious for malaria, to Tamu. Here there was already a growing number succumbing to the rigours of their march, to malaria and worst of all to the dreaded cholera. It was a repeat of the high death rate from cholera which took its toll of those who trekked from Prome across the Arakan Yomas; but they

144

were all natives of India and the safety of India was their irresistible goal.

As April dragged on, the vital part which the Chindwin fleet would have to play became more and more evident. Whichever route was taken in the British withdrawal to the Chindwin, the river would still have to be crossed. The Chittagonian crews now began to desert from the sternwheelers, but others from the Irrawaddy steamers were prepared to fill their places, and all eleven were running when on 30th April a Japanese force appeared on the west bank of the river opposite Monywa and cleared the defenceless town with mortar fire. Fortunately, all the sternwheelers were up river at the time and the Flotilla party at Monywa made for Alon, five miles north, and there intercepted the first downward bound ship; safely aboard, they made for Kalewa, stopping and turning round the remainder of the fleet as they were encountered.

The main British force, having crossed the Irrawaddy at Semeikon, had made for Shwebo and Ye-u, from where forest tracks were to be their route to the Chindwin. It was now a headlong retreat and a race for Kalewa, with two Divisions of British and Indian troops, and Burma Rifles, including the Armoured Brigade and such transport as had been saved, struggling to reach the Chindwin before the enemy — and before the rains broke.

More Flotilla men were now to show their mettle. Chief Engineers Jack Murie and William Hutcheon, commissioned in the Army for special duty, had been taking charge of ships when they were needed during the withdrawal up river. With crews of Chittagonian volunteers, ready to stay with a *sahib* they knew, they were now at Kalewa and were joined by others of the British staff keeping the six "S" Class sternwheelers, the largest of the Chindwin fleet, in commission for the task now before them. Thus began the ferrying of troops and vehicles to Kalewa from Shwegyin, a village on the east bank of the Chindwin some five miles down river. Shwegyin was the end of the "road" from Shwebo and Ye-u and there the Army began to arrive in ever increasing numbers.

Flotilla Assistant John Macnaughtan, then Lieutenant Burma R.N.V.R. released back to the I. F., was in command of this vital operation. Having carried out the Army's crossing of the Irrawaddy at Semeikon, he established at the Shwegyin/Kalewa crossing of the Chindwin yet another battle honour, nothing else could describe it, for the Irrawaddy Flotilla.

Hutcheon kept a brief diary, although they were running night and day and snatching sleep only when re-fuelling:—

> "7th May — General Alexander on board one trip today. Came up on flying bridge and had a yarn. Plenty of planes overhead and we are bombed — but he thanked me for a pleasant voyage!"

> "10th May — *Shillong* under fire from Japs — have to scuttle her. Kinnear comes in with *Sind* and takes us off. A lively morning. Transfer to *Sind* at Kalewa and ordered to return to Shwegyin for 48 Brigade, the rearguard, and told must get through at all costs. Meet Colonel Wheeler coming up by launch and turned back — the Japs are in Shwegyin now."

> "11th May — Asked by General Cowan to proceed to a creek about half way to Shwegyin and pick up troops. Made two trips, 1106 men first time, 1200 the second. Murie on this run too. On third trip I anchor off while Murie goes in for the last time, bringing off the Brigadier. We head for Kalewa — mercifully intact."

The Army was safely across the Chindwin at Kalewa and were now making for Tamu with all that remained of their transport. Light vehicles had been ferried over, but the tanks had to be left behind. The Flotilla party, with every steamer capable of running, and taking with them 48 Brigade, now made up river for Sittaung, 36 miles from Tamu. At Sittaung they scuttled the sternwheelers* and lost no time in starting their two days march, to be greeted at Tamu by General Alexander on 16th May with the news that he had awarded the Military Cross to Jack Murie in the field.

John Morton and his party of Assistants and Superintendents reached the Chindwin at Homalin nine days after leaving Katha. Many other Company men were on that route, Captains, Engineers and Chittagonians, and all were helped on that first stage of their long trek out to India by rigging up and using bamboo rafts on creeks running west into the Chindwin. But

---

*By a strange coincidence, taking part in this scuttling was Major Eric Yarrow, a Sapper officer and member of the Yarrow family who had built the sternwheelers — now Sir Eric Yarrow, Bart, Chairman of Yarrows.

there were long marches and the early acquisition of good boots saved many sore feet and no doubt lives too; every man of the British staff had long before equipped himself with army boots for the walk which had seemed inevitable at the end of the day.

At Homalin they were advised to make by boats for Tonhe, some 30 miles down river, and strike inland from there. Sittaung, another 30 miles on, was considered unsafe by then, 13th May, yet the Chindwin party did not reach there until the next day. But they were better safe than sorry and Morton's group set off from Tonhe on foot across the mountains to Manipur, a gruelling five days' march, climbing at times to 4000 feet. For over 100 miles they struggled on in the torrid heat, with still no monsoon rains, until from a mountain top they saw the plain of Imphal. The rains came as they approached the town of Imphal and soon they were being given the helping hands of relief workers.

The next day, 18th May, they were taken in a convoy of lorries 120 miles by road to the railhead at Dimapur and were overjoyed to find the Flotilla Chindwin party already there. Only the sad news that Captain George Garven, the Superintendent of Pilots, had died on the trek from malaria and exhaustion, dampened their high spirits. There were other casualties of the trek and of enemy action which were not then known, but in the main those few who had carried the burden of responsibility with John Morton were safe. No less than 550 units of the great Irrawaddy Flotilla of 650 vessels had been denied to the enemy. It was a sacrifice made with courage and honour in a unique epic of the British Merchant Marine.

Morton went to Chittagong as soon as he had recovered from his ordeal and set up arrangements for paying off crews. From a temporary office in Calcutta, and later at the Indian hill station of Simla, the Flotilla Company maintained links with the now exiled Government of Burma and with the Henderson office in Glasgow. Morton flew home in late summer, made his full report to the Directors and began the planning for a new Irrawaddy Flotilla after Burma was re-taken. Unable to obtain a flight back to India, he accepted a passage by ship and sailed from Britain in November, 1942. That ship was never heard of again.

So died John Morton. His name survives in the rolls of the Order of the British Empire, of which he had been made a Commander for the part he and his beloved Flotilla had played in that desperate British retreat from Burma.

147

PART TWO

INTRODUCTION

The calamitous events of 1942 did not mark the complete end of the Irrawaddy Flotilla, but to all intents — and certainly for the purposes of this book — they mark the end of the life story. Only as an epilogue can the years 1946 to 1948, when the attempt to re-build the Flotilla after the war was made, be acknowledged as having existed as part of that story; and so to an epilogue this period has been consigned.

In the chapters which follow, the authors have tried to bring the reader closer to their own experience of Burma's rivers, to some of the problems which were encountered in the running of the steamers, and to how these were resolved. And in recounting incidents which occurred long before they or the generation which they knew went to Burma, they have had the benefit of long memories for anecdote possessed by some of their contemporaries. The longest and most prolific of all belonged to Captain Hugh Chubb, whose own remarkable record of the many hundreds of river craft owned by the Flotilla Company in the 83 years of its existence was published shortly before his death in 1975.*

---

*The Irrawaddy Flotilla Company, published by the National Maritime Museum in Maritime Monographs and Reports — No. 7 (1973).

CHAPTER FOURTEEN

TAMING THE RIVER

1. By Conservancy

In 1824 when the "DIANA", the first steamship to ply on the Irrawaddy, navigated in these hitherto uncharted waters, danger spots were discovered the hard way and had to be memorized and related to some landmark. Countless riverside pagodas served this purpose, but not with the precision required to reckon a ship's position in an ever changing river.

The earliest record of marker buoys being used was by the Irrawaddy Flotilla in 1852 to warn their Captains of a number of dangerous places. By 1855 land beacons were added, their main purpose being to indicate where deep water channels crossed from one side of the river to the other. In those early days it was the custom for upward and downward bound ships to 'heave to' when they met to give Captains an opportunity to exchange channel information and keep themselves up to date with changing conditions.

As steamers using the river increased in numbers the necessity for planned river conservancy became more and more urgent. When the Irrawaddy Flotilla Company began, being the only organised transport operation on the river, it was taken for granted that the Company would assume full responsibility for river conservancy and this continued throughout its life, the service being free to all other users of the river. By 1870 the Irrawaddy was divided into beats, each patrolled by Burmese country boats hired by the Company to undertake the buoying and operated by their owners.

The country boat procedure was simple. A boat would be loaded with the readily available river sand to a required draught and then released from a point upstream of the channel to be marked to drift down close to one bank sounding depths as it went and placing buoys at shallow places. Groundings were frequent but refloating was simple when some sand was jettisoned, to be replaced immediately, and this enabled the boat to continue buoying until the downriver limit of the beat was reached. At this point the boat would be towed upstream again by the first upward bound steamer in readiness for its next downstream trip, which would be made close to the opposite bank. The arrangement sufficed but was very slow. The river could change too rapidly for the method to be wholly effective.

Much valuable information was learned from the country boat experience and it was used to help to decide the design of the first two Flotilla Company steam buoying launches to be built in the late 1870s. The *Echo* and the *Apollo* were each forty feet in length, drawing only about two feet draught and were the forerunners of many slightly larger and more powerful additions to the fleet in the years that followed. These little ships had the advantage that they could function in places where no other type of ship dared to go and like the country boat relied on sand ballast to extricate themselves from trouble when they grounded. As duty took them into treacherous waters, both engines and boilers were detachable to make salvage easier in the event of the worst happening. When larger ships grounded, the buoying launches were quite indispensable being capable of laying out anchors as well as buoying lead-out channels for them.

By the close of the 1880s the buoying fleet had increased to seven launches and by 1920 fifteen units operated the thirteen beats that spanned the eight hundred miles of the Irrawaddy from Yandoon on the delta to the northern terminus of Bhamo. These little ships were like miniatures painted in full Company livery, fascinating to watch at work with long bamboos made fast alongside, roofs laden with other tools of their trade and resembling a fully laden grass collecting boat such as one might see in the Fen district. In the high water season their services were superfluous, the fleet was withdrawn leaving only a skeleton service; and the important annual overhaul and docking undertaken then.

Nature, the cause of most navigational problems in channels, also provided the materials to master them. A buoy had to float and even when placed in fast moving currents must always extend above surface level to be visible from long distances. It also had to be moored to a river bottom of shifting sand. Early answers to these problems were simple and ingenious and with a few refinements remained unchanged down the years.

Bamboo, with adequate supplies available at many places on the river, was dicovered to be most suitable for marker buoys. These buoys, used in varying lengths between twelve and eighteen feet, depending on the strength of current and depth of water into which they were placed, were moored in such a way that when riding the current they remained aloft at an angle of about forty-five degrees and around eight feet exposed above the waterline. Each buoy was moored by a sandfilled gunny bag dropped into and soon embedded in the river bed and giving rigid anchorage. The base of each bamboo was attached to the gunny bag by liane or rattans, also found in plentiful supply at many places on the river. Buoys were painted to a code of colours which denoted their purpose, such as starboard and port, channel junctions and rock and wreck hazards. After the advent of ships' searchlights, a simple device was added in the form of a small bright tin disc suspended from the top of starboard buoys. These tin discs waved about gaily in the oscillations caused by the currents, giving bright reflections of the sun by day and the searchlight by night.

Much thought was given to directing river currents to create deeper leads on a falling river and before definite channels had time to cut themselves out. The problem was that in this interim period each year the diminishing currents had insufficient cutting force to sustain deep channels and the tendency was that the broad river lay placid with a uniform shallow depth. One method of encouraging deeper channels was copied from an idea used on an Indian river as early as 1836. Bandalling, named after an Indian Army Colonel Bandall, who conceived the idea, consisted of stakes driven into the river bed, skilfully sited across the river and laced with woven mats. This created a funnel through which the impeded water surged, scouring a deep water trough which became a navigable channel.

In the 1885 War, lessons were learned from the King's attempt to block the river at Ava to prevent the British advance by the sinking of ships, which actually resulted in better channels being created. On several occasions this expedient was used in attempts to improve difficult channels in later years, sometimes with lasting success, but more often than not such action had ill effect on other channels further down stream and the idea created more problems than it solved.

After each high water season the dropping river levels exposed the full ravages of erosion in the shape of huge trees and roots, which had been uprooted during submersion and deposited across the main channel to be. Eroded banks also left trees precariously overhanging the river at crazy angles. In 1887 the *Rescue,* a purpose-built paddle steamer, was commissioned and fitted with a jib crane and windlass capable of lifting snags up to forty-five tons in weight. A second post high water problem was outcrops of rock appearing in new channels scoured out during the flood conditions. For this particular job the stern wheel *Pounder* was built in 1904. Her speciality was to pound rocks in depths of up to eight feet of water with her bow 'pile driver' which was nosed with specially hardened steel teeth. She disposed of the resulting debris by means of a powerful pump.

Little conservancy was required in the delta as creeks, although narrow and winding, are deep. One troublesome matter was the accumulation of beda weed (water hyacinth) which thrived in brackish water and choked the narrow creeks. As changing tides prevented quick release to the sea where the weed died and sank, it became compacted and matted in the captive creeks, strong enough to support a man and an obstacle that sometimes disrupted the passage of steamers. An attempt was made to reduce this nuisance by use of a boom stretched across creeks to prevent weed from returning with ebb tides, but the task proved too great for this idea to be effective.

The use of lights ashore as landmarks for night navigation was never satisfactory, as they could be so easily confused with the many exposed lights showing from lonely river bank dwellings. But the dangers of night navigation in the delta in the high water season led to the introduction of lights as leading marks in 1922. Perhaps the most difficult place was where a narrow channel joined the broad river some miles north of Maubin, on the main route from the Irrawaddy to Rangoon, realistically known as 'Hole-in-the-Wall'. Near this point it was decided to place a land light as a lead-in and to appoint a local villager to keep it in trim and light the lamp every evening. This arrangement had its weaknesses where the frailty of the local human species became only too apparent. One day, finding that the path between his home and the lamp had become submerged, the lamp tender decided that his best action was to move the lamp. His initiative brought quick results; the first light of dawn revealed four night express steamers hard aground in the vicinity.

Most river blockages were caused by narrow sandspits forming across the mouth of deeper channels and in 1938 it was decided to experiment with the use of jet sandblowers to remove them. An old paddle steamer was fitted with a powerful water jet and, as a first trial, placed in a blocked channel to dissipate the offending sandspit. After working all night the first light of morning showed that the paddler was surrounded by dry land, a position from which she was ultimately able to extricate herself by means of her jetblower — but not before all existing channels in the neighbourhood had been worsened. There was some success later with this imaginative experiment.

Much was attempted and much was achieved in the endeavour to tame the everchanging river. The high cost of the buoying fleet and the pilot service repaid itself, not only in the safety provided but also by the better draughts to which steamers and flats could load in the low water season. The key man was the Superintendent of Pilots, who also controlled the buoying fleet. A senior and carefully selected Captain, his lonely tour of duty kept him continuously on the river for eight months every year, living aboard his own special steamer *Lanpya,* appropriately the Burmese word for 'pathfinder'. His reward was four months home leave each year, four months when the problems of the river, too much rather than too little water, he could do nothing about.

While the buoying and pilotage of the thousand miles of the Irrawaddy from Rangoon to Bhamo became and remained the responsibility of the Flotilla Company, the Government accepted responsibility for the Chindwin River from Monywa to Homalin, some 300 miles, on the principle that there was no road or railway beyond Monywa. All communication in the Chindwin area was waterborne. But the Flotilla Company provided the Chindwin Superintendent of Pilots on secondment, again a steamer Captain.

The sophisticated methods employed in the later years of the Company's existence, vastly different from the simple sand and country boat operation of the early days, were still not the ultimate in river conservancy. They had, however, to be geared to the revenues of the Company and how much these could stand for this essential, but expensive, service. When, in the 1950s, the Irrawaddy Flotilla was no more and the independent Government of Burma was seeking advice in many fields from Consultants from the United States, a survey of the river produced proposals which included the blowing up of areas of rock and river bank, the introduction of river training schemes and other immensely costly plans to improve navigation. Traffic on the Irrawaddy could not have paid for these grandiose ideas — no doubt they were right for the Mississippi — and none was adopted. In any case, they might well have done more harm than good, so fickle is the Irrawaddy when man sets out to tame its natural flow from mountain to sea.

2. By Navigation

Important as river conservancy was, the forces of nature had to be overcome by safe navigation and individual skill. The open ocean has its own problems, but the Irrawaddy navigator had a different range of perils, from raging currents to the shallows of the low water season. At both extremes he had to thread a safe passage through country boats and rafts that relied solely on the whim of wind and sail, the ineffectiveness of oars or merely unpredictable river currents. To watch a steamer being navigated was an experience always full of interest, enhanced by the often fairylike scenery; and the silence of night navigation took nothing from the scene. Stars and moon were plotted on the water as on a map of the firmament and in the delta areas further enriched by phosphorescence from countless marine organisms in the river and vivid fireflies on the river banks.

The sight of a main line monster — no other word can better describe a 20th century Rangoon / Mandalay steamer dwarfing as it did all other craft using the river — was always magnificent. With two cumbersome flats made fast alongside creating a unit beam measurement of 150 feet and a length of 326 feet, it was hard to imagine this ensemble making headway against currents of up to ten miles per hour. Swinging such a floating cavalcade into current to go alongside a ghaut or negotiating a dog-legged shallow channel, where only a few inches of water lay between keel and a blasted reputation, left no room for error. The confidence of the Captain and his skill were paramount; and these men knew their jobs. The main line Captain had to be on the bridge almost all the time a ship was under way; his Chief Officer, whose primary task was ship's cargo, could take only a sufficient part in the navigation of the ship to advance his own training for command.

Unlike the steamers on the Mississipi, which are controlled from a pilot house situated aloft, navigation was normally conducted from the bow area of the lower deck with an alternative position on the deck immediately above, which, when required, had the advantage that the navigator was above the searchlight beam at night. Some paddlers did have flying bridges right on top.

The first searchlights were introduced in 1886. Before that, night steaming, seldom practised, was entirely dependent on the kindly help of the moon. The type fitted to the Rangoon/Mandalay steamers were so large that they required two small motors to rotate them and, with an arc of ninety degrees, they were highly efficient. Stabbing a long sword of light into the darkness, every shadow was deepened, every reflection was intensified, and insects in the path of the light seemed to be the size of huge birds. The river scene stood out as in a flat picture up to several miles ahead and colours were vivid, with the green of the jungle and the white and gold of the riverside pagodas.

That first searchlight in 1886 was fitted to the steamer *Pekin* and the innovation was a double event, as the steamer also had a new type deep toned siren. Captain Beckett, with a taste for pageantry, decided to display the wonders of the searchlight on his first arrival at Thayetmyo and also to test the effect of the siren. Approaching the town at night with all lights dimmed except for his navigation lights, when he was abreast of the main landing place he suddenly put on all deck lights, sounded the siren and switched the searchlight on the town. His dramatic plan had far from the effect he desired. People fled in all directions, heading for the jungle and screaming that the big *'beeloo'* (devil) had arrived. It was several days before they would return to help unload the cargo from the ship and it was reported that one man died from the shock of the incident, while three women had miscarriages.

On one occasion a Captain accidentally broke the reflector of his searchlight and not wishing to report the matter, made an improvised repair. Obtaining a suitable piece of mirror bearing the words 'William Youngers Edinburgh Pale Ale', acquired no doubt from a Rangoon bar, he had it fashioned to the required shape and fitted. Shortly after, one of the Company's directors from Glasgow travelled on the ship when to his astonishment he observed the Pale Ale advertisement clearly etched on a white sand cliff on which the searchlight beam had been directed. A staunch teetotaller, he did not approve of the Flotilla Company advertising Mr. Younger's excellent product in the 'light' of his personal persuasion. A new reflector was fitted at the end of the trip — at the Captain's expense.

Very soon the searchlight became a standard fitment to all ships and made possible the introduction of the many night delta express services for which the Company was famous. In 1932 when the Twante Canal, the short cut from the main delta into the port of Rangoon, was opened, searchlights became compulsory there between sunset and sunrise for all vessels towing flats or cargo boats.

Contending with altering river levels, the river gauge at Bhamo was fully exploited. It took eleven days for a rise or drop in river levels to reach the upper delta area and steamer draughts could in consequence be predetermined before a ship left up from Rangoon. In the High Water season the danger was submerged river banks and flood currents with extended steaming times on the up passage.

But experienced Captains had other aids to navigation, such as ruffled water surfaces, shadows and river bank formations. They watched country boats struggling with the elements and there was little that escaped their notice. The country boats, aided by the prevailing winds to fill their sails and make way against the current, had an ingenious way of sailing down stream against the wind. It was their custom to put down a sea anchor or drogue, even a whole tree, which the effect of leading them only in the current where the water was deepest, giving unsolicited pointers to the wary Captains.

Not only could the navigator obtain the latest channel information from buoying launches, but he also had the help of pilots who accompanied ships over each sixty to seventy mile beat in which they specialized. Many of these pilots were Chittagonians, but there were also Burmese pilots employed by the Flotilla Company and earlier for the King's steamers. It is said that when one of the King's steamers was lost in the Second Defile in the mid 1860s the order went out for the pilot to be beheaded.

Rapidly changing river conditions, sometimes an hour or two could bring great differences, made it necessary for leadsmen to be sounding almost continuously during the low water season, except at a few quiet places where channels were straight and water deep. These men worked two hour shifts at the bow of the steamer or the flats that were being towed, making a change from lead and line methods to bamboo poles when dangerous shallows required more frequent soundings. Mark Twain glamourized the Mississippi leadsmen (the pseudonym itself means 'two marks' on the sounding line), but the Irrawaddy counterpart was outstandingly characteristic as depth readings were entoned musically, the descant changing to denote urgency. The Chittagonian call *'teen balm mila nahin'*, meaning three fathoms and no bottom touched, soon changed to specific depths being called, *'hath cum do balm'* (one hand less than two fathoms) and in greater urgency *'beelees cum ek balm'* (nine inches less than one fathom) as the water shallowed, followed often by a luckless bump as the vessel grounded.

There were channels habitually known to be dangerous, in which at some time or another there had been incidents that Captains involved were not allowed to forget. Such lasting testimonials of personal ignominy at the hands of nature often bore the specific Captain's name, making him famous in perpetuity. In this way geographical features became known as 'Beckett's Bluff', 'Clausen's Folly' and 'Sevenoak's Channel' to name but a few. Steaming down river in a very strong following current created problems and some channels, bedevilled by cross currents, a dog-legged turn in their centre and the presence of rocks, were virtually unnavigable and required a special procedure to gain passage at all. Here the steamer would be turned round above the channel to face the current and, by dropping a bower anchor, would actually pass down the channel stern first, relying on the added security of anchor and engines for control. With a narrow channel it was often necessary to take only one flat down at a time and, operating in highly disturbed water, only feet from rocks, the steamer seemed destined for destruction, which only experience avoided. There were occasions before channels cut out in the low water season when the river would be completely blocked, and on one freak instance was closed altogether for the passage of the largest steamers for six weeks on end.

Groundings were commonplace. Usually a huge wave would build immediately astern when a steamer ran into shoal water, which had the effect of lifting her even further into trouble once the hull was grounded. Occasionally groundings were sudden with a heavy impact, but more frequently on diminishing soundings smooth slow progress ended with a gentle slithering movement. This was most serious on a dropping river when, in a matter of an hour, the water could fall several inches, not to return to that level perhaps for weeks, even months. At these times all attempts to refloat had to be immediate, as failure could result in the vessel being high and dry in a few hours and with changing channels she could be stranded several hundred yards from the river itself.

It was an unhappy sight to see a steamer thus immobilized; in the case of the *Taping* in 1912 for nine long months and the *Momein* in 1919 for almost a year. On one occasion, when a steamer grounded at the top of an abnormally high river rise, there was considerable concern that it might be several years before similar conditions returned and it was decided by a system of wedging by degrees that the ship be lowered by eight feet to ensure earlier refloating. Partly for punishment, but more for security reasons, Captains or Chittagonian Masters of grounded steamers were forced to live on their vessels throughout the period of enforced inactivity, high and dry and usually miles from anywhere.

As it was always a laborious task to lighten grounded vessels quickly, an experimental ship was designed in 1939 to overcome this problem. The *Thumingala,* a twin screw diesel double decked vessel, was fitted with electrically operated ballast tanks capable of adding buoyancy forward or aft as the occasion required. This could well have been a blue print for future ship design had the Japanese War not ended her activities.

Natural hazards in the shape of rocks, snags, whirlpools and fog were there in plenty, but it was the man-made problems that were more frustrating to the steamer Captain. Fishing nets, supported by floats and controlled at each end by canoes, often floated downstream virtually from bank to bank closing the navigable channel and making it difficult for ships to go round them without having to enter shallow water. Teak log rafts composed of upward of 300 logs could be encountered in difficult channels with similar effect, and if they grounded whole channels could be altered and navigation endangered. But perhaps the greatest problems took place in the dark when happy-go-lucky Burmans would navigate their canoes, the only light showing being the glowing end of a cigar. With water hyacinth in the vicinity these could not always be picked out in a searchlight beam, and some incidents ended in tragedy.

Until 1931 there was no bridge over the Irrawaddy throughout its entire length. In that year the Sagaing Bridge was completed to carry the railway line through from Mandalay to

Monywa on the Chindwin and to the northern terminus at Myitkyina. This bridge, just short of a mile in length, had ten spans and it was the intention that all spans should be navigable for the largest river steamers. They had clearly not reckoned on river silting, as by 1942 only two spans could be used and then only with difficulty. The bridge brought another problem to the Flotilla Company. Not only was it necessary for the funnels of all the larger steamers to be shortened, but when the river gauge at Mandalay was 225 feet the clearance between ship and bridge could be as little as four feet. At anything over 227 feet the river would be closed to the largest steamers on the Rangoon/Mandalay services. Fortunately this happened only once, but the possibility was always present.

Taking a large steamer alongside a ghaut (landing place) was no mean feat of navigation. Each ghaut had its own peculiarities, from swirling currents to eddies actually moving upstream close to the bank. Going alongside followed a ritual. A mile or two away the ship's siren would be sounded, attracting not only the villagers attention but also the less welcome clusters of canoes and sampans eager for an early boarding, and children swimming out from the bank to enjoy the excitement of being close to the "monster". When positioned correctly above the ghaut, the anchor would be dropped out in stream and the bow eased towards the shore. To the Captain's command, four or five lascars, clad only in trousers, jumped overboard, the leader bearing in his teeth a light rope for his swim ashore, often in a swift current. With a footing established his companions assisted in heaving in the more substantial mooring cable attached, which they then made fast to a stout post placed for the purpose, or to a convenient tree. Once secured, the ship was allowed to swing astern and was manoeuvred into position alongside the ghaut by anchor and shore wire and finally made fast. The surging crowd would be making their way aboard even before the lascars had secured the gangways.

It is a tribute to the high standard of seamanship that so few serious accidents occurred during the history of the Company. From the beginning to the late nineteenth century period there were reports annually of losses on the river, some by fire, but most the result of strandings and the impossibility of salvage before a rise in the river level brought about heavy silting over the grounded hull. The pride of the fleet, *Thooreah,* the only three decked paddler ever built by the Company, and which had achieved some fame by carrying the last King and Queen of Burma into exile, struck a rock near Magwe in 1887 and became a total loss. She settled on her side and by the next low water season had disappeared under a huge sandbank which formed every year in the middle of the river between Magwe and Minbu. Fifty years later the top of the casings of her two funnels and some upper deck stanchions appeared above the sand. The Insurance Fund looked after these losses and later, when a loss became a rare occurrence, due to the improved buoying of the river, its successor, the Underwriting Account, grew to a substantial figure able to withstand any disaster short of war.

Loss by fire was not surprising in view of the highly combustible nature of some of the cargoes. Internal combustion caused several damaging fires, notably in consignments of groundnuts and cotton, and although a number of craft were burned out, since the turn of the century there were only two serious fires involving loss of life. One took place in 1904 at Nyounghla, the oilfield port for Yenangyaung, where the main line paddle steamer *Yomah* was burned out after a fire in a cargo of cotton. The second involved the steamer *Kashmir* on her maiden voyage from Rangoon to Mandalay in 1910. This was a costly fire, as the steamer and two heavily laden flats were completely destroyed at Dedaye, only a few hours steaming from Rangoon: the cause was put down to an oil fuel leak in the engine room.

An accident of a much more sinister nature occurred on 18th December 1928 when the tug *Ngatsein,* a steam vessel normally employed in Rangoon, had been sent across the Gulf of Martaban for special duty at Moulmein. During the return trip in the open sea, the tug developed a leak in the propellor shaft and the position quickly became serious. The ship was manned by a European Captain and Chief Engineer, supported by a Chittagonian crew. To assist the Engineer in the emergency, Captain Pinnington placed the Chittagonian Syrang in charge and proceeded to the engine room. While the repair was in progress much water was shipped and the panicking crew took to the only lifeboat, leaving the Europeans to their fate. Both men perished when the ship sank. Some time later the Chittagonians were picked up by a passing British India Company ship whose Captain, not satisfied with the explanation he was given, wirelessed the Police. In due course the crew were tried and the Syrang received a sentence of six months rigorous imprisonment.

It was the custom to employ elderly ships on ancilliary duties such as the towage of coal or firewood flats. It was on such a duty that the *Amherst* was engaged in 1924 when she holed herself on a pinnacle rock which pierced her hull and ripped plates apart from her bow to as far aft as the engine room. Although the flats that she was towing supported her for some time, the ship eventually sank. The unfortunate Syrang in command reported the accident to the Mandalay Agent by telegram in the following message:

"Steamer *Amherst* hit with brick and drowned in water near Kyaukmyaung — Nooras Jamal, Syrang."

No greater tribute was ever paid to the Irrawaddy Flotilla Captains than by V. C. Scott O'Connor of the Indian Civil Service. He travelled on Burma's rivers in 1904 and wrote in *The Silken East:*—

"And when the steamers come at night they fling their searchlights up the winding avenues and transform the world of dark trees, of swaying forests of cane and bamboo, of spired pagodas glittering with gold and of waiting people who appear as actors in a play, into a stage-land of extraordinary picturesqueness ... the lascars plunge into the flame-lit water and strain at the ropes as they race along the grass-covered banks.

"Three hundred feet and more in length, these steamers, and with flats in tow half as wide, they forge imperiously ahead as if all space belonged to them, swing round and roar out their anchor chains to come alongside, while the lascars leap and the skipper's white face gleams in the heavy shadows by the wheel — the face of a man in command.

"And when you see this wonderful spectacle for the first time you step on board the great boat expecting to find a man as imperious as his command, with eyes alight with power, and the consciousness of power, and the knowledge that he is playing a great part. But you find a plain man, very simple in his ways, with weariness written about the corners of his red eyes. Ah! they know their work, these men, if anyone does; and they do it, as the genuine sailor always does, thoroughly and without talk. And they run their ships with a skill and daring of which they are wholly unconscious. And I say nothing of the Clydesmen who rule the throbbing engines ..."

CHAPTER FIFTEEN

THE IRRAWADDY TRAVELLER

Before the British annexations Burma was poorly endowed with roads. Bullock-cart tracks usable during the dry season soon became impassable in the long months of the rains, and much of the population relied on the rivers for communication.

It was only by the opening up of the country with the introduction of river and rail services, and the building of roads, that any advance towards more modern standards of living could be made. At first this was a slow process in a land where simple existence was self-supporting with no problems from housing, built of plentiful bamboo for the taking, or food provided in sufficiency from river and field. But advancing development of the country brought bigger townships and markets and the greater need for intercommunication between them. Very soon the standard of life for the average villager became more sophisticated and refinements of life, which we now call consumer goods, became accepted basics in more comfortable living.

Traders of every description and people engaged in Government business were perhaps the principal travellers on the river services. Crop cycles in the various zones brought the movement of agricultural workers, Indian coolies in particular often using steamers in large parties as the seasons changed. The Burmese love of entertainment was satisfied by the continual movement of *pwé* parties and their followers, who constantly toured the various towns attracting many other travellers to their performances. The popular Pagoda Festivals were events attended by thousands of eager and excited pilgrims, who often journeyed for long distances to be present. And the ubiquitous itinerant *hpoongyis* (monks) with their yellow robes were to be seen on almost every steamer.

Many travellers were involved in some form of Government business, from officials to members of the public concerned with litigation in the District Courts. Some Districts could control as

163

much as 200 square miles, thus involving litigants and witnesses in long journeys to reach the Courts and the problem of arriving during the few hours of daily sittings. Ferry services, many with daily sailings, were planned to cater for Court times, the most important being the Prome/Mandalay Service, operated by fast paddle steamers, unencumbered by flats in tow, connecting daily all riverine District headquarters on that 300 mile stretch of the main Irrawaddy. This Court service was repeated on all other parts of the main river, the Chindwin, the delta and in the Moulmein area.

On a river of swift currents and levels varying as much as forty feet between high and low water markings, the question of boarding and landing passengers sometimes presented problems. Piers being out of the question, the only satisfactory solution .was the use of dumb craft which could be moved between high and low water locations, sometimes up to four miles apart. Elderly steamers and flats proved particularly suitable for this function as they also provided covered space for cargo, quarters for offices, and in some cases, a local Agent's residence. At wayside villages, too small to justify a dumb landing craft, steamers went alongside the river bank; and where this was not possible cutters were used, or, in delta areas, the sampan filled the gap.

Well-appointed first class accommodation was provided on the larger passenger steamers, the cabins being fitted with beds and not the more familiar ships' bunks. First-class quarters always occupied the forward portion of the upper deck, using the extreme bow section as a promenade deck which gave an uninterrupted view of the river ahead. The lay-out of the accommodation behind the promenade section was simple, the open space containing the saloon and dining room and the cabins opening out from either side of this area. On smaller steamers, with the exception of the crack Rangoon to Bassein Night Express, the only alternative to deck travel was a screened-off portion forward on the top deck which provided privacy, but no bedding or messing, and was aptly described as 'the Screen Berth'.

It was customary for Europeans in Burma to have the traditional early morning *chota hazri,* a large late breakfast, afternoon tea and a late dinner. First-class menus on the steamers gave a very wide choice. Madrassi butlers, who controlled saloon activities, were capable and amiable; but although they spoke English they often required the assistance of the Burmese steamer clerks to write the menus. At times this gave cause for amusement. A passenger once commented, "Following a meal of gargantuan proportions sufficient to tax the capacity and digestion of a python, the menu concluded with the words 'God save the Passengers'." On a paddler one Christmas Day at Prome an unexpected party arrived on board to share an inadequate supply of turkey. The butler, on being questioned how he had made everything go round so well, made no secret of the fact that he gave plenty of turkey to gentlemen who were not drinking and a mixture of turkey and fowl to those who were and less able to discern the difference.

Many notables travelled on Company's steamers. As has already been told, King Thebaw and his Queen were conducted down the river from Mandalay in the *Thooreah* on their way to banishment at the end of the Burmese Monarchy. In 1889 H.R.H. the Duke of Clarence travelled by the then new paddler *Beeloo* but nothing surpassed the splendour of the river journey by the *Japan* in 1906 when the Prince and Princess of Wales, afterwards King George V and Queen Mary, travelled down river from Mandalay to Rangoon. Captain de la Taste, then Commodore of the fleet, was in command; the hull was painted white and the funnel yellow for this particular occasion. The Crown Prince of Siam also travelled with the Flotilla in 1906, appropriately in the *Siam*. Not until 1937, at the time of separation from India, was another steamer provided for distinguished visitors to Burma. The Marquess of Linlithgow, Viceroy of India, then paid a farewell visit, and travelled from Prome to Mandalay by the *Mysore*.

It was normally the Captain's duty to finance messing costs on his ship. On the occasion in 1886 when the steamer *Mindoon* was taking the Viceroy of India (Lord Dufferin) to Mandalay, it was discovered that the Viceroy was very partial to ox tail soup and, being at Prome at the time, the Captain gave orders for the purchase of twelve ox tails. While no expense was spared to ensure the comfort of his important guests it was with some consternation that the Captain later discovered that twelve complete oxen were on board.

The entire upper deck on these large paddlers, with the exception of space taken up by First and Second class accommodation, was open and available for deck passengers. These would appropriate a section of deck on which they would spread their mats and bedding, and barricade themselves in with their belongings which usually included their food for the voyage. This could be augmented by a stallholder who supplied light refreshment such as tea, sweet drinks and sweetmeats. A water pipe with pump on the lower deck supplied all personal needs, including ablutions, and for easy access was placed prominently for all passers-by to see. Burmese women are extremely modest, but bathing presented no embarassment: for they never bathe without wearing a *loongyi* (long skirt), tucked under the armpits, below which the cleansing is conducted. Ablutions completed, a dry *loongyi* is put on over the wet garment which is then allowed to fall to the ground.

With the Burmese taste for bright clothes, deck passengers presented a colourful scene. Often travelling in their Sunday best, their spotless clothes still showed the ironing folds and displayed their fine silk garments to great effect. Males, attired in their colourful *loongyis* and *gaungbaungs* (headgear), matched the females in cleanliness, but lacked only the daintiness of feminine charm and varied immaculate hair-styles.

Burmese women gave endless attention to the combing and doing up of their hair and would sit before a tiny mirror in full view of all other deck passengers. Female toilet was a lengthy process, as it often included the application of a face powder or paste made from *thanaka* bark and applied for the dual purpose of cosmetic and protection from the sun.

The common sight of parties of prisoners being transferred from courts to prison, accompanied by their police escorts dressed in their drab khaki uniforms, was a contrast to such colourful scenes. It was customary for convicted prisoners to be chained together in groups; and while this undoubtedly increased security it had the effect of lulling the escorts into complacency, so that they were often seen asleep in the heat of the day. On more than one occasion prisoners were known to have had to awaken their guards to draw their attention to the fact that they had arrived at their destination.

With nothing to do but sit on deck, talking or eating or sleeping, while a steamer was under way, most passengers indulged in two of the national habits, "a-smokin' of a whackin' white cheroot", and chewing betelnut. Burma is famous for its fine black cheroots, but the local country type is a very different proposition. This white cheroot is a fearsome contraption sometimes measuring one foot in length with a diameter of over an inch. The outside covering is composed of maize leaves, giving the white appearance. This is stuffed tight with what looks like chopped hay, but is, in fact, cheap tobacco leaf mixed with herbs previously boiled in palm sugar. Part of the smoking ritual required a pot: partly to provide a resting place for the cheroot while it was handed round for others to share, but more practically as a safety measure, for they were prone to burst into flame, showering sparks over nearby passengers. The shared smoke was indeed communal, and included even babies at the breast, who were often seen being given their chance to have a puff.

The chewing of betelnut is an unpleasant habit to Western eyes, but the very bitter taste appeals to the Eastern palate. Betelnut ready for chewing is a mixture which contains betel vines, slacked lime, areca nut, tobacco, cutch (a resin) and various spices all rolled up in leaves which are neatly cut with special trimmers ready for use. The chewing is followed by the spitting out of a scarlet expectorant which dyes the mouth, lips, teeth and tongue of the chewer. On the steamers it left indelible stains when it landed on teakwood decks.

The Company lay wide open to fraud. There was always danger that tickets might not be issued, or wrongly punched; and that passage money collected would never reach the ships' accounts. Crews, operating in distant parts of the river, particularly in the delta creeks, were tempted to defraud the Company. But Inspectors and junior Assistants were there to grapple with devious habits, the latter making surprise boardings while ships were under way. The Company realised that swindling could never be wiped out altogether and the policy was based on suppression to ensure that it was kept under control. This problem was mainly confined to steamers commanded by Chittagonian syrangs, fine fellows in so many ways, but often tempted to make a little on the side.

Having gained valuable experience from touring in service steamers, the junior Assistant graduated to his own Inspection Touring launch which became his home for tours sometimes of months at a time. For added mobility a Speed Boat *Rover* capable of 32 knots, was kept in tow and regularly used.

Inspection launches were constantly on tour in the delta, and a vigorous 'bush telegraph' kept Syrangs of service steamers well informed of their whereabouts. Good intelligence was very much on the side of Syrangs as there were many places where services converged in the network of numerous creeks and information could be passed on. It became something of a battle of wits, but this is not to say that every Syrang was dishonest: far from it, but there were some among the large number employed who had to be watched. One of the advantages of the *Rover* was its ability to use narrow creeks, off the map so to speak, and proceed undetected at high speed to a distant place where, unsuspected, a really surprise boarding could be made.

Often lying for hours, hidden in jungle foliage just off a service route, the *Rover* would wait ready to pounce when the steamer came along. Boardings were made at full speed either from directly ahead or astern of the 'victim'. When approaching from ahead the *Rover* depended on a crash 180 degree turn, using the steamer's bow wash as a pivot and often being alongside before the steamer's engines could be stopped. In all cases the Assistant had to make a jump-boarding, which could be dangerous but gave no time for ships' records to be put in order if swindling was in progress. It was an exciting life for the young Assistant, out on his own on the delta. This, of course, was not all that he did. Agencies had to be inspected, the general conduct of the services watched, firewood contractors dealt with and traffic kept under close scrutiny.

The element of surprise was exploited to the full when on one occasion an Assistant made a long seaplane journey to check a ship at a secluded place north of Mandalay. This type of exercise, and indeed the very presence of Assistants, went a long way towards prevention. The constant war against swindling was pursued relentlessly and resulted in 'catches' sometimes involving scores of passengers travelling without tickets. But in general, crews dared not run such risks, for the penalty when caught was instant dismissal.

Checking of tickets and questioning passengers could be frustrating, however well Inspector or Assistant spoke Burmese; and it was difficult to keep such examinations relevant to the task. Passengers could be shielding a dishonest crew, or were perhaps merely anxious to include as much of their personal background as possible in their responses. Obtaining tickets for the check was not always easy. For this operation passengers could be divided into different groups. First there were those who did not know where they had put their tickets and therefore could not find them. Next there were those who thought they knew where they had put their tickets, but still could not find them. Then there was the distrustful citizen who kept his ticket in some secret place which required a long search for recovery. There were also those who had temporarily moved down to the lower deck for social or toilet purposes and had left their tickets on the upper deck. Finally there were some who had actually lost their tickets through misadventure of having them blow overboard.

The cardboard ticket when journey-punched had serrated edges. Elderly male passengers often wore jackets with many pockets both inside and outside the garment, all of which had to be searched before a ticket was recovered. Others had fancy inside pockets large enough to accommodate a watch but small enough to catch all the punch marks on the ticket, preventing it from being extracted in one piece without almost dismantling the jacket. Matchboxes were for some reason considered to be safe places to keep tickets, but frequently in strong river breezes both matches and tickets were blown overboard when tickets were being presented. It was also common to find groups of passengers who kept the family tickets in their *tiffin* carriers (food containers), sometimes immersed in the wet contents for added safety, but illegible and sticky when handled. Dainty Burmese women with pocketless *eingyis* (muslin jackets) often kept their tickets skewered to their tight under-bodices by a safety pin which gave added security if the pin was rusty. But at least they knew where their tickets were.

Indian coolies had different problems. They kept their valuables tied up in the two long ends of their *dhotis*, which they tied tightly round their midriffs. When their tickets were requested they would unwind one of the ends, a prolonged process, to discover only their money, the ticket being enshrined in the other end making it necessary to repeat the whole performance. It was a great relief for the inspector when confronting a Military Police Havildar who would have tickets at the ready and pronounce clearly: "There are five in our party and here are the tickets".

Births on board were not infrequent; and at one time when the Company offered a reward for such an important event they increased greatly in number, leading to withdrawal of the offer. But the Burmese sense of fun was seldom absent. When a child was born later on one of the steamers, loud laughter was heard from behind the hastily erected screen when the mother was asked if she had yet purchased a ticket for her ten-minute-old offspring.

The travelling public were open to the dangers of dacoity, fortunately on rare occasions. Main Line steamers carrying European Captains and Engineers were unattractive to would-be dacoits, but on the delta, where the smaller passenger steamers under the command of Chittagonian Syrangs plied the lonely jungle-shrouded creeks, the danger was greater. Dacoits would board a vessel in the guise of fare-paying passengers and at a prearranged time and place they would produce their hidden arms, intimidate the crew and passengers, and run the ship ashore where other members of the gang lay waiting in the jungle. The hapless passengers would then be stripped of their money and jewellery and the hijackers would disappear into the maze of creeks and swamps.

There was one incident where the dacoits were not so fortunate. A cargo barge was left unattended while the crew of two proceeded to a nearby village to buy rice. During their absence the dacoits lay in wait. When the crew arrived back the dacoits were mystified to see them halt on the deck and after much animated conversation and gesticulations take to their heels in the direction of the village. The coast now being clear, the dacoits boarded the vessel and entered the hold. Almost immediately, however, a half grown tiger sprang at them killing one of the intruders with a single blow and dragging his body away. The terrified survivors managed to clamber ashore, only to be confronted and arrested by a headman with shotgun who had come out to investigate the crews' report.

The Company was not without rivals on the Irrawaddy. The Burma Rivers Transport Company was formed in 1908 with Indian capital and supported by the Indian-owned Rangoon Oil Company. Within a period of two years, their fleet had grown to twenty two steamers and twenty flats and they not only went into the oil business but were carrying passengers on the main river. To meet this serious threat the Flotilla built two $15\frac{1}{2}$ knot special steamers *Otaru* and *Osaka* with the sole purpose of shadowing this competition and depriving them of passengers. For some months the battle raged, but the more speedy Flotilla steamers soon convinced the opposition that this competition was not worth while and the B.R.T. fleet was purchased by the I.F. Company in 1911.

The enterprise of Indian merchants also led to "defensive" acquisitions of two small fleets of creek steamers in 1916. G. H.

Irrawaddy Flotilla Company head office building in Rangoon, by floodlight; built 1933

Rangoon/Mandalay Express paddle steamer *Nepaul*, 326 feet in length

Chittagonian lascars swim ashore with the mooring line.

Kalewa, Chindwin River, scene of the crossing in 1942 of the retreating British Army. Flotilla sternwheeler at ghaut

Clamouring to board the Bhamo Bazaar Steamer.

Irrawaddy Flotilla Company Executive Staff, 1947 (key to the photograph at Appendix III)

Acha and Company and Ghulam Hussein, both of Bassein, were operating no less than eighteen single and double decked launches in the Bassein district to the extreme discomfort of the Company and there was no alternative but to purchase both fleets and add them to the Flotilla. But in the delta the field never remained clear for long and acquisitions were expensive, so the policy thereafter was to engage opposition in rate cutting battles hopeful that they would go away to some less lucrative locality. The Company were quick to move when their services were challenged by others. Yet competition in the delta continued, mostly by one launch owners, but nonetheless unwelcome.

Moving up to nine million passengers a year was a giant undertaking. This was half the population of Burma in the 1930s. The delta areas alone, upward of 5000 square miles, crossed by an unascertainable number of tributaries and minor creeks, had an intricate system of passenger services, and it can be said that every creek leading anywhere had Company steamers plying on it. The area was served by fifty-seven different services and employed a fleet of over one hundred double decked creek steamers, and ten single deckers used in very narrow creeks.

Little wonder that the young Assistant was bewildered at the veritable maze of creeks when first assigned to delta touring. It took many months to acquire a full understanding of the steamer services and of the topography of the Irrawaddy delta, but once acquired he soon became well acquainted also with the Irrawaddy traveller, the Burman in his natural surroundings.

CHAPTER SIXTEEN

STRANGE CARGOES

Some idea of the diversity of cargo carried by the Flotilla can be gained from a Company pamphlet published in the 1930s. It gives the following very brief description:

"Great bales of cotton, bags of rice, blocks of jade, lacquerware, silk, tamarind, elephants sometimes, woven mats, maize, jaggery, bullocks, marble Buddhas, oilcake, tobacco, timber. In upward bound cargoes will be found all the various imports from Europe; motor cars, corrugated iron, condensed milk, matches, aluminium ware, sewing machines, piece goods, soap, cigarettes, cement and whisky."

Burma is an overwhelmingly agricultural country with liberal rainfall in all but the dry central zone, and had great untapped potential until the British consolidated the territory into one unit after 1885. Dry and wet zones, each with different indigenous crops, created the necessity for transport to move produce from one to the other.

Dry zone crops, typical of which were groundnut, teelseed, peas, beans and cotton, made an important contribution to the agricultural produce of Burma. Groundnut and teelseed, valuable in their natural state, had the added value in that they had high vegetable oil yield and after processing provided almost sufficient for Burma's internal requirements. Myingyan and Pakokku were situated in the centre of the richest growing area and much of the processing took place in these areas. Groundnut cake, yet another by-product, was a useful export and much of it found its way to the United Kingdom to be used as cattle feed.

The cotton trade, based near the centre of the Dry Zone, produced fine quality cotton which was an important export and was one of the basic items moved across the Tengyueh Trail from Bhamo to China. Ginned cotton is used extensively by the Chinese for the quilting of their light clothes as protection against winter cold. Much of this cotton was sent by Flotilla steamers to Bhamo, where bales were split up on the riverbank into suitable sizes for mule loads for onward despatch. Yunnanese blacksmiths eagerly purchased discarded iron bands taken from the cotton bales and with their forges on the foreshore converted them there and then into splendid swords which accompanied other merchandise into China.

Paddy, the main crop of the Wet Zone, accounted for 70% of the country's total agricultural output and between the World Wars placed Burma as the largest exporter of rice in the world. By 1934 Burma had an exportable surplus of over three million tons of rice, upon which Madras, Bombay and Calcutta greatly depended. In the earlier years much paddy was transported to Rangoon from the delta paddy fields to be milled in the highly mechanised European owned mills there. As time went on, although increased production fully employed the Rangoon mills, the situation changed with more and more paddy being milled closer to the fields in which it was grown and this resulted in the mushrooming of many small mills all over the delta. This suited the Flotilla Company, as the shipment of clean bagged rice direct to ocean ships in the ports was much preferred to bulk paddy loads.

Burma depended almost entirely on the import of manufactured goods. Although very heavy and bulky items were often carried on steamers, no cranes were fitted; the loading and unloading could be adequately handled by plentiful labour using wedges or bamboos as circumstances required.

The special enchantment of Irrawaddy cargoes, however, was to be found not so much from ordinary local produce but from strange and unusual items which reflected national characteristics and unfamiliar treasures extracted from mines or nature herself.

Mandalay, the great distributing centre for Upper Burma, with its monastic associations, was one of the chief centres for craftsmen who fashioned all kinds of Monastery furniture and adornments, sculptured images, inscribed slabs, Burmese jewellery and art. Perhaps most common of these were religious monoliths, emblems and trappings; evidence enough of the great reverence that the Burmese have for their Buddhist faith. Small marble images of Buddha were frequently shipped and their fascination was enhanced by the variety of the three postures to which they were fashioned. All had their religious implications.

The seated version indicated meditation, the standing, preaching, and the recumbent the attitude of death or attaining *'Nirvana'*. Although Buddhism is the main religion of the Burmese, 'Nat Worship', which it replaced, is still very much adhered to and 'nat shrines' are to be seen everywhere. Constructed of bamboo and highly decorated, these were often carried on board the steamers in various stages of completion and usually surrounded by curious spectators. Occasionally effigies of 'gryphons' or *Chinthés* seemed to set the scene in the legends of ancient Burmese history and bring alive the inherited romance of the people.

The artistic produce of the land abounded everywhere, but in terms of colour few items compared with the intricately designed Pagan lacquerware made with horse hair and bamboo, usually in a mixture of vermilion, yellow, green and black. Lacquerware containers of all shapes and sizes and for all domestic purposes were distributed throughout the land.

Before the turn of the century the advantages of a mobile 'bazaar' river service was recognised to bring to smaller towns and villages the facilities normally enjoyed in the market shops of larger communities. Such a time consuming undertaking could not have been achieved successfully on Express services; it was obviously a task more suited to a slower schedule. The 'Bazaar' system was first introduced on the Rangoon/Mandalay run and extended later to Mandalay/Bhamo where, operating in that more remote and sparsely populated area, it provided a real necessity.

Fortnightly the Bhamo Bazaar steamer, towing its double decked flat, sailed from Mandalay on its five and a half day journey upstream. The upper deck of the flat and the steamer was permanently partitioned off, providing stalls from which stallholders sold their goods on display to eager villagers at every shop. Stallholders were private individuals not employed by the Company; they remained permanently on board, often handing on their right to their children when they died. This arrangement enabled them to build up business connections as they became well known in every village on the river. Company administration was simple; the freight paid was determined by the total load leaving Mandalay and charged for the round trip. There was no question of complaint at such an arrangement as stallholders were free to bring back unsold cargo without question and enjoyed much greater profit if they did not. These stallholders not only traded the items they displayed on board but also accepted orders to be delivered on subsequent voyages; a profitable business to both stallholder and Company.

The arrival of a Bazaar steamer at a village on the Bhamo run was an event of great local importance, not only to the village but also to other villages for many miles around. The distant sound of the steamer whistle was the signal summoning the entire population to the riverbank and the place would come alive in an almost festive atmosphere. As the ship berthed, and before gangways could be placed, the chatter and laughter increased to a roar as villagers jostled for favourable positions to obtain a quick boarding. With stalls on board tightly packed together, back to back in the centre of the upper decks of steamer and flat, the narrow space remaining for walkways left little room for the throng of enthusiastic customers to move about. The situation was made more chaotic by the inborn custom of intense bartering over prices, which had to be conducted in screams to be heard above the general babble. But the first warning whistle for departure brought even worse clamour and the crescendo in noise reached panic proportions as everybody hastened to conclude their transactions. Fortunately good humour and laughter smoothed over any incidents in the lemming-like disembarkation that preceded actual departure and the restoration of peace in the village again — until the next Bazaar steamer.

There was considerable movement of livestock by river. Seasonal paddy ploughing in the delta required the long distance haul of bullocks and buffaloes from Upper Burma in huge numbers, often in flat loads at a time.

The carriage of elephants presented problems and became specialised traffic. The average Asiatic elephant, being over eight feet in height and weighing about three tons, is a considerable bulk to persuade into confined spaces. Not all elephants can swim or like deep water or strong currents and they were often ferried across the river in steamers. Occasionally large numbers of elephants, which may have been purchased in Thailand, or herds being transferred between distant teak forests, were moved by ship over long distances, and in such cases special flats were used.

The Company's first lesson in handling elephant traffic took place in 1884 when six elephants had to be ferried across the Irrawaddy at Prome. To achieve this it was decided that a passing Rangoon/Mandalay steamer would drop its flats and undertake the one mile crossing single handed with the elephants. A freight charge of one hundred rupees per animal was agreed. Having reached the opposite bank the elephants were duly unloaded into shallow water and with obvious relief filled their trunks with water and generously sprayed themselves and each other. Returning to Prome the steamer sounded her deep toned siren to announce her arrival and hearing this in the distance the elephants raised their trunks, and in 'mating' response, trumpeted loudly and followed the steamer back to Prome. Although this story is authentic, it is not known how the question of freight charges was resolved.

This was not the only time that ship sirens had an effect on elephants. In 1886 the new steamer *Canton* was experimentally fitted with a new 'chime' siren. This siren, the forerunner of a modified equivalent used thereafter on the larger main line ships, had a disturbing effect on the elephants working in the Dunnedaw Sawmills of the Bombay Burmah Corporation in Rangoon — they knocked off work every time they heard it. The value of this particular siren was appreciated by the Bombay Burmah so much that it was sold to them as a timekeeper and remained in the Mills for many years.

The Burma Government enforced rigid rules for the protection of wild elephants against unauthorised hunters. In an incident in 1894 a steamer Captain spotted an elephant on a nearby river bank, and, being a good marksman, took aim and killed the animal. He stopped his ship and went ashore to examine his prize. He found to his consternation that the elephant bore the letters 'F.D.' on its rump, and there were six links of chain attached to its left hind leg. It was the property of the Forest Department and cost the Captain the suspension of his gun licence and a fine of £60. This incident resulted in the Forest Department making it illegal to fire at any animals from moving steamers.

The initiative of Captains was certainly tested when it came to shipping elephants. In 1909 several elephants were being transported by flat in the upper reaches of the river and Captain Taylor dropped the flat where required and proceeded with his steamer single handed on his voyage. At his next call the Captain received a telegram stating that one of the elephants had fallen through a wood covered hatchway of the flat into the nine feet deep hold beneath. The Captain sent a telegram back to say that no attempt should be made to rescue the elephant until he returned, but ordered the Burmese Agent to have every able bodied man, woman and child in the village nearby ready with baskets, buckets or anything which would hold earth or sand. On his return Captain Taylor instructed the assembled villagers to keep filling their receptacles with soil or sand close to the flat, carry this aboard and tip it into the dark deep hold — but not on top of the elephant. As the earth and sand went in, the elephant, shuffling about by instinct, trampled it down and eventually the level rose to that of the deck and the elephant was able to walk out and join the others.

Although the transportation of elephants by river was not a regular occurrence, from as early as 1908 a specially adapted flat, able to carry twenty-four animals, was always kept ready. This flat was designed to meet and overcome the problems of the movement of elephants. The first requirement was a specially strengthened deck to support abnormal stresses such as stampedes brought on by a thunderstorm, a ship's siren, or the sudden noise of steam when boiler pressures were reduced at the close of a day's journey. Indeed, for this latter reason, it was customary to tow the elephant flat on the port side of the steamer to be remote from the engine cylinder drains.

The elephant flat had a four-inch teak deck superimposed. Elephants suffer extreme discomfort when standing on a hot steel deck, and this could cause their feet to swell, making it necessary for fetters to be removed, which would be a dangerous operation. Under corrugated iron roofing, temperatures could soar, and piped water was supplied to keep decks and animals cool. Electric lights replaced the kerosene lamps which normally lighted flats.

Elephant handlers, the *'oozie'* in Burma, were fully employed under way, arranging fodder, looking after their charges, and ensuring that tusks were not damaged if the animals became restive. The Burman likes to watch elephants; and sightseers flocked to the river bank when an elephant flat was reported, making it advisable to anchor midstream or some miles from a town or village. Even there, the flat would be visited by canoes; but there would be less disturbing noises than when lying alongside at a town.

By far the most difficult problem was the loading of elephants into a flat. Stubborn and suspicious by nature, they took badly to unfamiliar experiences, and great patience was required to get them on board. It was not only necessary to construct a gangway of sufficient strength, and without gradient: it had to be heavily camouflaged, including roofing with banana leaves, to give the impression that the tunnel thus constructed was merely an avenue leading to luscious jungle beyond. Any water visible through the gangway would bring operations to a halt. The process could take days, but once a leader could be coaxed to move across the gangway the others readily followed. Once on board, it was a question of security of fetter and chain; and the phase of settling down began. Plenty of green fodder seemed to calm the animals: before long there would be no noise except the heavy munching of sugar cane and kaing grass, the low rumbling, and the tonk of contented trunks being lightly and playfully struck against the deck of the flat.

Unloading was generally a much easier matter. Like released prisoners, the elephants did not require to be told that their hour of freedom had arrived. They followed each other down the gangway with purposeful gait creating a scene in the imagination that one might associate with the unloading of Noah's Ark.

The traffic carried by the Flotilla was not only the pulse of trade on the river, but also, by its sheer volume, an indicator of trade in the whole country. In short, the fortunes of the Irrawaddy Flotilla, almost wholly dependent on the cargo and passengers carried, swung to the same pressures which determined the trends of Burma's fluctuating economy.

CHAPTER SEVENTEEN

REFLECTIONS ON THE RIVER

The enchantment of the Irrawaddy varies almost mile by mile. Rangoon was a cosmopolitan city in the time of the British, not on the main flow of the river at all but on one of the lesser delta outlets to the sea. But this enchantment begins there, if only for the fact that the flat delta lands for many miles around are dominated by the magnificent Shwe Dagon Pagoda, the greatest pagoda in the land and perhaps in the world. And Rangoon was the gateway to Burma when Michael Symes made that first pioneering journey into the little known country in 1795; it remains the gateway today.

The coastline fringe of the delta, extending inland at places up to forty miles from the sea, is a multitude of creeks bounded by mangrove growth whose twisty roots overhang the muddy swampy banks. They bear the slimy evidence of succeeding tidal levels and provide a haven for a great variety of marine life. There is little firm dry land in the mangrove swamps, which renders exploration impossible in a roadless morass, except by canoe. Phosphorescence by night both in the water and from insects on the banks brings the waterways alive. Alligators, not plentiful but present, lurk in dark narrow creeks. The navigable creeks are a naturalist's paradise, each bend quite likely to reveal something of interest, from pelicans, storks and hornbills to numerous other unusual waders.

The wide estuary of the Bassein River can be stormy in the monsoon season, stormy enough to have made it necessary for the Flotilla steamers operating in the area to be boarded up for safety. In these parts fishing is the main occupation of a sparsely inhabited area and in water frequented by large species of fish from the Bay of Bengal, including particularly venomous water snakes, catches are varied — and often dangerous.

Sailing through the narrow creeks affords the opportunity to see both nature and village life at close quarters. The ever present paddy birds, as the egrets of Burma's ricefields are known, are as much part of the scene as the fields themselves, with their white plumage and stately movements. The peaceful Buddhist monasteries set among the village trees, with their distinctive architecture and temple bells tinkling faintly in the breeze, create an atmosphere of quiet, disturbed only by the barking of pariah dogs and the sounds of village life. By night the croaking of frogs and the clicking of the cicadas are incessant, with the noise of the evening gossip and laughter from the village groups never far away.

A few miles north of the delta town of Maubin, the first stop on the Rangoon / Mandalay steamer route and reputed to be the home of the largest and most lively mosquitoes in the world, the main Irrawaddy is joined and from then northward the land becomes firmer and the river broad. Although towns rely on man-made bunds for their protection against flood, sandbank formations in the low water season now encase the main channels of the river and the high earth banks are often far from the channels. Horizons are seldom without a gleaming pagoda and a distant clump of tall trees indicates a village beneath.

Donabyu, a small town just over 100 miles from Rangoon and scene of General Bandoola's last battle of 1826, is typical of many up and down the river, although it has a special activity in the manufacture of the world famous Burma cheroots. At the first light of morning the town is astir and soon the cultivators set out for their fields with their bullocks. Girls fill jars at the nearest well to provide the daily household water requirements. Hpongyis, clad in their bright saffron robes and in the shade of their parasols, file out from the monasteries barefooted, with novices carrying the begging bowls to receive their daily food. The bowls are rapidly filled as they go from door to door accepting gifts from the ever magnanimous people. Activity on the river banks springs to life as fishermen commence to remove their overnight catches from net and line and proceed to rebait for the coming day. In towns such as Donabyu where there is a market the whole scene is enlivened by bright and colourful clothing, less evident in the little villages where there are only common work-day chores to be performed in the fields. In the monasteries, where children are taught to read and write, they commence studies in the early morning. Under the direction of the hpongyis they can be heard from the river ghaut chanting the alphabet loudly in unison and learning the characters of the language and texts of their faith. There is little or no illiteracy in

Burma. The children are sometimes grave and dignified, but ever with laughter peeping from their dark eyes; and the gracious way in which they help their old people leaves no doubt that Buddhism gives the Burmese a philosophy of family care which is quite exceptional.

Just over 100 miles north of Henzada, quite suddenly, the first real riverine contour is encountered at Ghautama Hill where a cliff of some 300 feet bears down on the west bank of the Irrawaddy and extends for about $1\frac{1}{2}$ miles. Here is a navigational danger in the high water season when the fast flowing river drives into the precipitous bank. But most notable about this imposing cliff are the hundreds of sculptured images of the Buddha carved into niches in the rock, depicting incidents in his life. Many of these sculptures are gilt or white painted, a unique sight for the river traveller.

The town of Prome is situated in richly wooded country on the east bank of the river and was the centre of ancient history dating back two thousand years in legendary recordings, when it became the seat of the Tagoung Dynasty of Burmese Kings. Prome boasts one of the largest pagodas in Lower Burma; set back from the river on the summit of a hill 138 feet high, the Shwesandaw towers another 180 feet skyward in commanding majesty and beauty.

In the long reaches north of Prome the river meanders past the small town of Kama. Here, as though giving a welcome to Upper Burma, two magnificent giant Chinthes (the Burmese mythical lions from which Orde Wingate took his Chindit emblem in the war against the Japanese) stand sentinel side by side on the river bank, pure white in striking contrast to the darker trees in the background. These emblems of Burmese history are to be seen at their best at sunset against the brilliant colours of a changing sky as the sun sinks behind the distant western mountains; and in the East it leaves no time for twilight in its haste.

From a steamer approaching the oil centre of Yenangyaung comes the sight of an abrupt contrast, like the lights of a great seaport. The tall trees of the south are replaced by a forest of oil derricks which monopolise the skyline. And in the light of dawn this arid oilfield area presents a landscape of drained, exhausted and colourless terrain.

Sixteen miles north of the oilfields, as if by magic, the industrial scene is left behind and at Pagan there is a return to the eleventh century. Rich in colour and steeped in history, Pagan is perhaps the greatest showpiece of Burma. Once there were thousands of pagodas there. Even now the entire countryside is covered with them; and there are still many hundreds, a score of which are bigger than St. Paul's Cathedral. Inspiring structures, the famous Gawdapalin and Ananda Pagodas have been particularly well preserved, although other great pagodas built much later at Ava and Amarapoora are now in crumbling ruins.

Nowhere is the Irrawaddy more imposing than in the broad reaches where it flows past Pakokku, Pagan and Chauk. At dawn over this wide stretch of river, as the sun climbs back into a new cloudless day, opalescent reflections appear on the water as morning haze disperses. The huge cone of Mount Popa rises from the plain in the distance and remains dominant on the skyline for the entire course of this hundred mile sweep of wide river. Popa, a 5,000 ft extinct volcano of text book shape, rises some seventy miles east of the river from the seemingly endless expanse of the plain. The crater, the centre of Burmese 'nat' worship and legend, is a mile in diameter and the thick forest trees and bushes on its floor are the home of hamadryads in plentiful numbers. Seen from the river, distance tints Popa dark blue, adding colour to the panoramic view of the vast hazy plain.

There must be few finer approaches to a city than to Mandalay where the river flows between Ava and the pagoda-crowned ridge of the Sagaing Hills*. Beyond to the north-east lie the picturesque outlines of the sacred Mandalay Hill bedecked with white and golden pagodas interconnected by white painted masonry stairways. Behind lie the brooding mountains of the Shan plateau. Mandalay is the centre of Burmese art and history. Of the city itself the most distinctive feature is the Fort; surrounded by a high battlement wall of red brick the enclosed area is a precise square each side being $1\frac{1}{4}$ miles long; outside the wall lies a continuous 100 ft wide moat. Twelve gates provide access to the enclosed area and although the wall was temporarily breached in several places in the Japanese War, it still stands as it was built by King Mindon. Contained within the walls of the Fort lay the King's Palace, the Centre of the Universe to the Burmese; but unhappily destroyed in the War.

In this setting the river road to Mandalay ends.

North from Mandalay we have already seen that the river enters a new world, passing through wilder and more sparsely

*The Sagaing Hills are depicted on the book jacket.

populated country. At the entrance to the Third Defile fifty miles above Mandalay there is a small island in mid-river named Thihadaw on which stands a unique pagoda and monastery. Even at the time of Simon Hannay's first journey to Bhamo in 1835 Thihadaw had changed from earlier days when hundreds of pilgrims attended the annual pagoda festival. Then it had boasted lavishly gilded spires and much grandeur; by 1835 it had long since fallen into disrepair with the golden domes only a tarnished reminder of the past.

Thihadaw was also well known for a large species of catfish which had been tamed over the ages by the hpongyis of the monastery. Dr. Anderson, the naturalist who accompanied the Sladen mission to China, wrote in his diary that these fish came to be fed when they were called. Provided with rice and bananas Anderson went off in a boat to the island. The boatmen began calling out to the fish until they were seen cautiously approaching the bank; when the food was thrown to them they eagerly devoured it, rising out of the water until not only their uncouth heads but also their backs protruded. Anderson even stroked their backs as they remained poised for more food! But this phenomenon had receded into the past by the time steamers of the Flotilla began to ply the waters of the upper Irrawaddy.

Thabeitkyin lies in the middle of the Third Defile on the east bank and is the riverine station for Mogok, some 70 miles in the mountains to the east and connected by road. Mogok produces the finest rubies in the world and here was a political problem in days gone by, a problem resolved at the beginning of the seventeenth century when the Burmese King seized the territory from the Shan State to whom it originally belonged.

Of the Second Defile much has already been written. It will always be the most striking memory of the Irrawaddy to be taken away, a memory of the sheer majesty of the scene which it presents to the river traveller. And if he has seen the eerie panoramas it can create in the cold weather season of early morning fogs he will never cease to wonder if it was all really true. The fog may clear on the river above and below this defile, but still cling all day to the precipice above the channel; and the steamer can pass from bright sunlight into such darkness that the searchlight may have to be used to pick up leading marks.

The navigable part of the river for the Irrawaddy Flotilla ended at Bhamo. Set in beautiful mountain scenery there is still much evidence in Bhamo of the Chinese influence; and the hill peoples intermingle there, bringing to the market unusual commodities — much of it contraband. Opium, from the poppy fields of China in the Yunnan Province only seventy miles distant, has always been a problem in the area. The use of opium was forbidden by the Kings of Burma and by the British Government, but in the British time, shops were set up and supply allowed to addicts who would otherwise have died. With the constant arrival of caravans from the Tengyueh trail, whatever action the Customs and local police applied smuggling and intrigue took place; and no doubt still does.

For nearly a hundred years the Irrawaddy had its Flottila. Even now, the very existence of this period of British ships and men on their river will be largely forgotten by all but the oldest of the riverine people. To those few British who were there and still survive, the enchantment of Burma and her rivers is an ever present memory, a memory of their good fortune to have known this unique and beautiful land, and its people.

EPILOGUE

On the 3rd of May 1945, leading elements of General Slim's XIVth Army re-entered Rangoon. As Slim wrote in his book *Defeat into Victory*, "the population in thousands welcomed our men with a relief and a joy that they made no attempt to restrain. We were back!"

Those Burmese who had worked in the old days for the British, whether in the administration or the Companies, were overjoyed at the prospect of returning to their jobs and resuming their associations. Many of their British friends and former employers were actually with XIVth Army, and there were some moving reunions. With commendable speed, the Army formed a number of agencies to get the administration on the move again, concentrating on essential supplies and transport services; and these were manned by the old hands, who were transferred from their combatant units to form the nucleus of a Civil Affairs Service. One of the agencies thus created was the Civil Affairs Service (Burma) Inland Water Transport, and into this were drafted British, Burmese and Chittagonians from the "Old Flotilla". Several of the river services were soon running again, with the help of such few craft as had been recovered and could be made serviceable, supplemented by powered vessels brought in by the Army. By the end of 1945 the Civil Government was in full swing, the last individuals had been released from military service, and the Irrawaddy Flotilla Company was back in business, with Stuart Macdonald as General Manager in Rangoon.*

But the optimism was fated to be short. It was obvious that the new generation of Burmese political leaders, which had helped in the closing stages of the war to expel the Japanese, had not done so with any thought of bringing back the British. As the year 1946 passed and the shattered economy of the country began once more to take shape, the Burmese leaders left nobody in any doubt of their aspirations. Early in 1947 they went to London, and returned with a promise of independence within a

*Stuart Macdonald. another product of Patrick Henderson and Company. had joined the Flotilla Company as an Assisatnt in 1927.

year; and on the 4th of January 1948, the Union Jack was hauled down for the last time at Government House, Rangoon.

The ideology driving the new Government was strongly nationalist and strongly socialist, and its leaders had made clear even before independence their intention to nationalise the Irrawaddy Flotilla and the British Timber Companies. In June 1948 the Burma Government took over the Flotilla Company, and christened it The Inland Water Transport Board. A few paddle steamers still ply on the Irrawaddy these thirty years later, but they are few and far between — and very old: the diesel engine and propellers have replaced steam and paddles.

As we have seen throughout this narrative, the Burmese have never taken kindly to having foreigners on their soil, although many close and treasured friendships have developed between individuals. The nationalisation of the Companies, which gradually extended to all foreign enterprises, meant the disappearance of the British, and many who came away were sad to leave the country in which they had expected to spend their working lives. Since those days, both Stuart Macdonald and Alister McCrae have revisited Rangoon and been warmly welcomed and lavishly entertained by former staff and colleagues. But Burma has once more withdrawn into her shell. Except for a well-worn tourist track from the Shwe Dagon Pagoda at Rangoon to Pagan and Mandalay there is little freedom of movement for the foreigner.

The Union Jack no longer flies over Government House in Rangoon, for the Head of State now lives there. But it flies over a certain house in Signal Pagoda Road on the outskirts of the city; a graceful building with a broad teak staircase of shallow treads, and a beautiful garden. Now the residence of the British Ambassador to Burma, it was known by generations of Flotilla Company men and their wives as *Belmont,* the house of their General Manager. On ten acres of land bought by George Swann in 1885 the Company built five houses for their British staff, the first timber *Belmont* being replaced by the present Residence in 1927. Now all the houses are homes for the British Embassy staff; but they remain a lasting symbol of that great enterprise which contributed so much to those halcyon years of prosperity in Burma.

[For use of SHAREHOLDERS *only]*.

THE IRRAWADDY FLOTILLA
AND
BURMESE STEAM NAVIGATION COMPANY,
(LIMITED)

Incorporated under "The Companies' Act, 1862," by which the Liability of each Shareholder is limited to the amount of his Shares.

CAPITAL £100,000—in 2,000 SHARES of £50 Each.

FIRST ISSUE £60,000, IN 1,200 SHARES OF £50 EACH, OF WHICH £30 PER SHARE IS AT ONCE TO BE CALLED UP.

Further Calls will be made as required for the purposes of the COMPANY, at intervals of not less than Three Months from the date of any previous Call.

DIRECTORS:

T. D. FINDLAY, ESQ. (MESSRS. T. D. FINDLAY & CO.), Glasgow.
PETER DENNY, ESQ. (MESSRS. WILLIAM DENNY & BROTHERS), Dumbarton.
ROBERT HENDERSON, ESQ. (MESSRS. P. HENDERSON & CO.), Glasgow.
WILLIAM DAVIE, ESQ. (MESSRS. J. J. MUIR & DAVIE), Glasgow.
JAMES NICOL FLEMING, ESQ., MERCHANT, Glasgow.
JOHN M'AUSLAND, ESQ. (MESSRS. DENNY & CO.), Dumbarton.
JAMES GALBRAITH, ESQ. (MESSRS. P. HENDERSON & CO.), Glasgow.

BANKERS:

THE CLYDESDALE BANKING COMPANY, GLASGOW.

SOLICITORS:

MESSRS. MOODY, M'CLURE, & HANNAY, GLASGOW.

AGENTS AT RANGOON, MAULMAIN, AND BASSEIN:

MESSRS. TODD, FINDLAY, & CO.

OFFICES AT GLASGOW:

15 ST. VINCENT PLACE.

This Company has been formed for the purpose of taking over a purchase recently made by Messrs. TODD, FINDLAY, & CO., of Rangoon and Maulmain, from Her Majesty's Government of India, of the Flotilla of Steamers and Troop Vessels hitherto engaged in Government service on the River Irrawaddy and connected therewith a Contract made by the former with the latter, for the sole conveyance of all Government Passengers, Goods, and Specie on that river, thereby securing the general Mercantile traffic, now very large and yearly on the increase. It is also intended to join with this service that of the general Steam traffic between Rangoon and Maulmain, and the Towage service in the Rangoon and Bassein Rivers hitherto worked in part by the Steamer "Ava," (which Steamer will be taken over by the Company), and to extend operations in connection therewith as may afterwards be deemed judicious.

A Memorandum of the Steamers and Troop Vessels is annexed; these will be transferred to the Company as at the First day of January 1865 at the very low price at which the purchase was made, adding the expenditure since in repairs and general overhaul, — the whole amounting to £20,000. The Steamer "Ava" will be taken over as at same date at the price of £12,000 — the original cost of the Steamer placed upon the Station.

The Contract with Her Majesty's Government of India (above referred to and now in working operation) is for a period of Five Years, from May 1864, and the remunerative nature of the traffic is evidenced by the result of the first Six Months working of only three of the Steamers of the Flotilla, leaving a profit of £3,860, or at the rate of £38 per cent. per annum on the original cost of the Flotilla. The net earnings of the "Ava" for the same period realised £2,445, being £40 per cent. per annum. These Six Months, it may be mentioned, are during the S.W. Monsoon, when the traffic is much less than during the other Six Months of the Year.

The Agency of the Company at Rangoon, Maulmain, and Bassein, will be in the hands of Messrs. TODD, FINDLAY & CO., and Messrs. P. HENDERSON & CO. will (under the supervision of the Directors) conduct the working of the Company's affairs at Glasgow.

IRRAWADDY FLOTILLA.

STEAMERS—	"Bentinck,"	. . . 300 Tons, 90 Horse Power.
	"Nerbudda,"	. . . 300 Tons, 90 Horse Power.
	"Damooda,"	. . . 250 Tons, 60 Horse Power.
	"Mahanuddy,"	. . 250 Tons, 60 Horse Power.
TROOP VESSELS—	"Sutlej,"	. . . . 200 Tons, '
	"Paulang,"	. . . 200 Tons,
	"Bhagerutty,"	. . . 200 Tons,
STEAMER—	"Ava,"	. . . . 341 Tons, 80 Horse Power.

Managers in Burma of the

IRRAWADDY FLOTILLA COMPANY LIMITED

(Incorporated in 1876)

1876-1884	George G. Swann
1885-1896	Frederick C. Kennedy
1896-1902	James G. Findlay
1902-1906	James P. Hay
1906-1911	Randolph J. Wilkinson
1912-1919	John A. Polson
1920-1927	Robert Sinclair
1927-1932	W. T. Henry
1932-1937	Thomas Cormack
1937-1940	A. T. McCreath
1941-1942	John Morton
1943-1946	T. E. Brown
1946-1948	Stuart T. Macdonald

Irrawaddy Flotilla Company Executive — 1947

Back (l. to r.)
W. G. STUART (Asst. Engineer Superintendent), U BA BWA (Assistant), J. C. IMRIE (Assistant), U SOE MAUNG (Assistant), R. C. FULLARTON (Assistant), A. S. PRENTICE (Assistant), A. DAVIDSON (Accountant), S. C. LIU (Assistant), U BA CHAN (Assistant), W. W. MACKINLAY (Accountant), R. A. PAXTON (Assistant), CAPTAIN H. W. ROWLEY (Asst. Marine Superintendent).

Middle
CAPTAIN JOHN REID (Marine Superintendent), Wm. MILLER (Assistant). J. M. MACNAUGHTAN (Asst. General Manager), S. T. MACDONALD (General Manager), ROBERT BORLAND (Director on visit). A. G. McCRAE (Deputy General Manager), A. S. KINNEAR (Assistant). H. CRAWFORD (Assistant), W. J. L. HARRIS (Engineer Superintendent).

Front
U TAW (Assistant), ROWLEY MORRISON (Assistant), U HLA BAW (Assistant).

Assistants absent upcountry
K. R. GOURLIE, SAW PO HLA, N. MITCHELL, J. H. GEMMELL.

Sources

Embassy to Ava Sent by the Governor-General of India in 1795 — by M. Symes. Mitchell Library, Glasgow.

Journal of a Residence in the Burman Empire — by H. C. M. Cox 1821. India Office Library & Records.

Michael Symes — Journal of his Second Embassy to the Court of Ava in 1802. Edited by Professor D. G. E. Hall and published by George Allen & Unwin Ltd. in 1955.

Journal of an Embassy to the Court of Ava in the Year 1827 — by John Crawfurd. India Office Library & Records.

A Narrative of the Mission sent by the Governor-General of India to the Court of Ava in 1855 — by Henry Yule. Mitchell Library, Glasgow.

A portrait and description of Thomas Spears. India Office Library & Records.

Doctor Clement Williams' survey of the Upper Irrawaddy in 1863. India Office Library & Records P/437/71.

Paddy Henderson — by Dorothy Laird. A history of P. Henderson and Company, 1834-1961, published by George Outram and Company Ltd.

Paper by Captain Edward Sladen on his 1868 expedition to Bhamo and across the trail to Tengyueh, read to the Royal Geographical Society in 1871.

Paper by Annan Bryce, Manager of the Bombay Burmah Trading Corporation, read to the Royal Geographical Society in 1886.

Minute by Colonel Edward Sladen of August 1885 — from *The Times* of 1st January, 1886.

Burma Military Proceedings 1885 — P.2433. India Office Library & Records.

India Military Proceedings 1886 — P.2768. India Office Library & Records.

The Lacquer Lady — by F. Tennyson Jesse. The story of Mattie Calogreedy (alias Fanny Moroni) published by William Heinemann Ltd. in 1929.

Canoe to Mandalay — by Major R. Raven-Hart, who also travelled by steamer (circa 1938) and acknowledges the "kindness of Captains and Engineers and Agents of the Irrawaddy Flotilla, and of the I. F. itself."

The Pagoda War — by A. T. Q. Stewart, published by Faber & Faber in 1972.

INDEX

193

GUERLAIN PARURE.